W9-AHF-270

the God of All Comfort

Donna Pyle

Eight Lessons about Hope in Christ Based on 2 Corinthians 1:3–7

A Women's
Small-Group
Bible Study

CONCORDIA PUBLISHING HOUSE · SAINT LOUIS

Published by Concordia Publishing House
3558 S. Jefferson Avenue, St. Louis, MO 63118-3968
1-800-325-3040 · www.cph.org

1 2 3 4 5 6 7 8 9 10   21 20 19 18 17 16 15 14 13 12

Thank You...

To *Luanne*, for giggles, accountability, loving Jesus outrageously and contagiously, and showing me how.

To *Doug*, for sharing your sideways humor, leading with a servant heart, and allowing God to redeem and use your broken pieces to profoundly impact my life.

To *Kristin*, for gracefully asking tough questions that God used to heal my heart.

To *Joel*, for intense integrity, speaking the truth in love, and letting your yes mean yes.

To *Roxanne*, for standing in faith instead of falling in fear.

To *Jennie*, for ending your sentences with exclamation points and making a difference in my life and the lives of children.

To *Hannah* and *Ashley*, for letting hope and the love of Jesus shine so brightly in and through you.

To *Heather*, for your amazing blog and insights on addiction and grace.

To *Lindsey*, for your tender heart, passion to follow Jesus, and grace-filled care of those you love.

To *Ray*, for sharing honest feelings with compassionate grace.

To *Janetta (Hoot)*, for your ninja editing skills, wicked humor, and boundless encouragement.

To *Sherrie*, *Lisa*, *Annie*, and *Bre*, for belly laughs, gut-level honesty, Starbucks runs, loving Jesus tenaciously, and enriching my life beyond measure.

To *Salem's worship planning team*, for your invaluable input and servant hearts.

To *Rachelle*, the best literary agent on the planet.

To *The Coolios*, the most amazing community of Christian writers, for your hearts like Jesus, writing expertise, and calming words when God turned me upside down writing this study.

To *Lisan*, *Monica*, and *Toni*, the most amazing sisters and best friends I could ever ask for.

To *Mom*, for lavishing on me unconditional love and compassion so much like Jesus.

And most importantly, to *my Savior;* my life would be rubbish without You.

Table of Contents

Forward

Christmas decorations hang forgotten. Wheezing cats snooze nearby, whiskers and paws twitching. Fingers type a staccato beat into the night. The keyboard's M is barely visible from wear. Soft music breaks the loud silence. The fireplace blaze reduces to embers as the dramas unfold.

As I complete writing this Bible study, I'm thanking God for this privileged loneliness. This self-imposed solitary confinement is necessary to translate interviews revealing soul-scarring events. Essential to capture. Difficult to articulate.

Theirs and mine.

The history of real pain. The drama of spiritual struggles. Stories of anger, misplaced expectations, fear, abuse, loss, and betrayal. They shout for space on the pages.

And God whispers into the chaos.

Comfort.

Bruised lives redeemed by a faithful Healer. Hope offered by a murdered Messiah. Restoration secured by a risen Savior. "For as we share abundantly in Christ's sufferings, so through Christ we share abundantly in comfort too" (2 Corinthians 1:5).

No one likes suffering, yet there's healing in the telling.

Abundant comfort.

As the laptop screen glows long into the night, gratitude overflows as I recall the faces of these story-sharers. The profound impact they've had on my spiritual journey. Honored by their trust to reveal great pain redeemed by an even greater God. A holy experience. And I'm already praying.

For you.

For the lives He will touch by these studies written around their stories in light of His Word. For the shadowed hearts He will usher back into His glorious light through them.

And somewhere in these stories, I pray you find yours.

Pouring amazing grace through the chapters, God gushes His love into our empty wells. Faithfully demonstrating how His life-giving Word works healing in us. Received, His soothing comfort then offered through us. Despite our discomfort.

If we let Him.

Introduction

In the midst of suffering, comfort often surprises us. A kind word. A soothing hug. A special delivery of the Savior's love. Right where we stand. Right when we get blindsided.

In the middle of hurt.

On the main street of chaos.

In the vortex of life's storms.

We all need comfort and compassion because life gets tiring, does it not? When we struggle with sin, when family members aren't saved, when bills stack up unpaid, work exhausts us, our health fails, and loved ones hurt.

Discouragement easily seeps in.

God desires something infinitely better for us. Nothing touches our lives that He has not filtered first. But discouragement robs us of peace and contentment. If it hangs around long enough, doubt, despair, and depression join the pity party.

Suffering causes us to forget our blessings and look only to our circumstances—especially if we suffer over a prolonged period of time. It creates distaste for the present. Dissatisfaction with the past. Distrust of the future.

But when we view our difficulties from the balcony of faith, we rest in God's assurance that He never leaves us unloved or uncared for. God's hope shines as a beacon of comfort.

Hurt blinds us to yesterday's blessings, causes indifference to today's opportunities, and creates insecurity regarding tomorrow's provision.

Over these eight lessons, our journey will take us through a section of Scripture titled "The God of All Comfort," in 2 Corinthians 1:3–7. The apostle Paul, the author of that letter and an expert when it came to suffering, offers insight and encouragement that God is not blind to our troubles.

God is also not necessarily concerned about our comfort, at least the way you and I define it. He's concerned about our character. So to burn off the dross, He hands us the blast goggles of His Word and lets loose His refining fire in our lives. He burns away pride, ego, arrogance, self-centeredness, and everything else that inhibits His work in and through us.

Some days we feel crispy fried. Other days, we find hope and renewal shooting up green through a scorched heart.

In order for us to be able to relate to comfort from many different scenarios, I interviewed seven faith-filled Christians who relied on timeless truths to walk in obedience despite loss and heartache. Through their stories and God's amazing Word, we follow the unmistakable footprints of a loving Savior who turns scars into life-changing stories.

This handful of ordinary people originate from very different backgrounds, yet use their extraordinary experiences to shine a God-sized floodlight on a compassionate Savior who weeps when we weep.

Let me warn you, these stories aren't pretty. Loss, betrayal, shattered trust, anger, misplaced expectations, abuse, cancer, fear, divorce, and sacrifice bleed onto these pages. Followed quickly by love and hope provided by God, who relentlessly pursues us with ultimate comfort.

We need the God of all comfort.

As these stories unfold and we dig deep into Scripture together, God's encouragement pours over us as we behold time and time again how He moved, rescued, and restored good from bad.

God redeems our stories through His story.

If you have suffered, needed comfort, and craved compassion, this study is for you. Over these eight lessons, you will learn about a Savior whose mercies arrive new every morning. Comfort that surpasses what our eyes see. Compassion offered by One who suffered most of all.

This study will encourage you.

You may be going through a difficult, painful storm in life right now. You might be resting in the calm following one. You may see storm clouds on the horizon. But pain is a chapter, not the book. In the midst of pain, God engraves His love on your softened heart as He adds your story to His history of faith-filled warriors.

You may feel a sense of hopelessness in your situation, but God reminds us that we have hope and a future with Him. As we study these Scripture passages about comfort, grace, and love, God whispers reminders into our souls of His promise to bring good out of every situation. Even the one you're experiencing right now.

This study will challenge you.

Perhaps you could offer college-level classes on comfort because you strive to maintain it at any cost. You don't like risk. Life is vanilla. Comfortable. Safe. You've traded your position on the spiritual battlefield for an observer's box in the stands. You dodge the fiery darts of spiritual warfare, hiding behind those actively engaged. You don't care who gets hit. As long as it's not you.

God wants more for you.

This study will re-ignite your passion.

Perhaps life has dealt you so many painful blows that you've given up. You've checked out of relationships. You've stopped going to church. You see the negative side of every situation first. You don't remember what joy feels like.

Yet Jesus pursues you in love. A Messiah who died so you could live fully alive.

This study will change your focus.

You may be angry with God because you cannot figure out the reason for your pain. You've been good. Lived an upright life. Served Him faithfully. Tithed and given generously.

But instead of allowing God to guide your situation, you focus like a laser on one question: *What can I do to make things better?* Self-centered, works-based focus has closed your mind to the unconditional love and purposes of God.

God-based focus strengthens us. When our spiritual eyes rest on Him, we receive His guidance and comfort. He enables us to offer encouragement to others. Helping those around us takes our eyes off of our troubles. We receive His comfort so it flows through us to those who hurt.

Keeping our eyes on Jesus is key.

LESSON 1

FATHER OF MERCIES

Even in the Fire

Blessed be the God and Father of our Lord Jesus Christ,
the Father of mercies. 2 Corinthians 1:3

When the uniformed officer pulled into her driveway, Jennie knew time was up.

How could 20 minutes have gone by so fast?

That's all the warning she'd received. And it had expired. She had to leave.

Now.

She and her two daughters haphazardly packed the minivan with all the worldly possessions they held dear. There wasn't time to be neat or organized. The danger raged closer. Mandatory evacuations had been ordered. For the first time in her life, she was fleeing to save their lives. It just seemed so surreal. Thick smoke choked out the midday sun. Huge flames appeared in the distance. The sound of exploding pine trees jolted her senses. Smoldering ash carried on high winds forewarned a deadly scenario. The Texas wildfires were out of control, destroying everything in their path. The lethal inferno headed directly for their home.

How do you prioritize your life in twenty minutes?

Jennie struggled to focus through panic and fear. She called her brother-in-law to enlist much-needed guidance. She needed to organize her things. Grab important papers. Call a friend to ask for shelter. Find both cats, who had disappeared under the beds when they sensed chaos.

And the whole time she prayed: *Lord, please help us. Preserve us. Protect those trying to save us.*

Reminding herself to walk with purpose instead of run in panic, she gave her daughters urgent instructions. Twenty minutes seemed to go by in seconds. But when the officer arrived, she had to leave immediately, whether or not she had grabbed everything they needed. They rushed out the door and flung themselves into the minivan. The dense smoke blanketed the sun in an eerie red glow.

It looked like hell had taken over.

The policeman shouted for Jennie to leave. He had to warn others, corral panicked livestock, block roads, and direct approaching firefighters. As she slid the key into the ignition, she met the eyes of her daughters. The anxiety reflected there matched her own. With a reassuring look, she backed the minivan down her driveway.

Jennie, Hannah, and Ashley didn't know if they would ever see their home again.

They arrived safely at her friend's home and settled in for the night. Jennie just kept praying: *God, please find a way to let me know one way or the other if my home is still standing. I cannot bear not knowing.*

She slept fitfully. Rising early, she wandered into the kitchen. Her friend was listening to the news as she made breakfast for them. Jennie sat down at the kitchen table as thoughts bombarded her mind. *What next?*

She turned toward the television and froze.

The news reporter stood in the middle of charred remains, relating the destruction caused by the wildfires. But Jennie's eyes were riveted to the swing set in the background.

That's ours! It's not burned!

Joy began to fill Jennie. Then the camera panned out. Where her house should have stood there lay piles of ash. Pieces of metal. Fragments.

O God, help us. Thank You for finding a way to let me know. But—now what?

Although the massive fires affected thousands of lives, it felt personal to the core.

Difficulties always do.

Where do we find comfort when our world turns upside down?

We desperately need the Father of mercies in that moment.

Day 1

Refining Fire

Emotions feel raw after such a traumatic event, so Jennie emphasized to her daughters that they were facing this as a team. They would deal with whatever came along as a team. And they were moving forward as a team. One day at a time.

Have you ever known people with the ability to comfort others despite personal tragedy? They face seemingly overwhelming odds or heartbreaking loss with a calm demeanor and purposeful steps. As we look on in amazement, we wonder at their secret.

On the other hand, some people feel devastated by personal hardships. They find no peace or consolation as they fall apart at the seams.

Where do those comfort givers find the strength to move past their suffering?

The apostle Paul was one individual who learned that secret, and he passed it along to us in his second letter to the Corinthians.

1. With what words does he start out in 2 Corinthians 1:3?

_____

_____

Although Paul experienced great suffering, persecution, and opposition in his ministry, he begins the letter by praising God. Paul realized that even in the midst of hard times, God, who brings grace and peace, is worthy of our worship.

2. When you face difficult times, are you still able to praise God?

_____

_____

3. What does offering God praise look like in your life?

_____

_____

Rather than starting with the problem, Paul begins 2 Corinthians 1:3 by identifying the Problem-Solver: "the God and Father of our Lord Jesus Christ." Paul never shunned God's refining fire. When he struggled with a personal weakness—a thorn in the flesh—he still affirmed God's faithfulness with a thankful, worshiping heart. With tenacious faith, he relied on God's promise to provide guidance and strength for his times of trial.

4. When you endure trials, do you rely on God as tenaciously as Paul did?

_____

_____

You and I operate in a very capable culture. Advances in technology place the world's information at our fingertips. When we experience difficulties, we're more likely to turn to computer search engines for a quick answer instead of patiently waiting on God to provide guidance and direction.

But computers cannot provide us the strength to endure.

The grace to be kind.

A love that forgives.

When trials exceed our spiritual or emotional capacity, search engines offer cold companionship. Instead, we need to swallow our pride and learn dependence on God. When we trust God and His leading, we receive His comfort.

5. How do these verses demonstrate living a life dependent on God?

2 Chronicles 14:11

_____

2 Corinthians 1:9

Second Corinthians is an intensely personal letter from Paul. False teachers had levied attacks against his character and the integrity of his ministry, so he used strong words to defend, correct, and teach. Yet he did so with great compassion. He wrote 2 Corinthians out of a godly love for those who had gone astray. Compassion represents a vital ingredient in establishing relationships.

6. According to Isaiah 54:10, what two things does our compassionate God say will not be removed?

God's covenant of peace and steadfast love brings us comfort. From a human perspective, showing compassion most often occurs up close and personal—in our space, so to speak.

Compassion is something we *feel*.

Comfort is something we *do*.

One cannot be genuine without the other. Relationships become uniquely important in our times of suffering because we receive comfort and compassion at a deeper level from those who know us best.

If you are enduring a difficult season now, translate that to your own situation for a moment.

7. Are you more open to receive comfort from a close friend or an acquaintance? Explain.

An acquaintance may attempt to comfort you, but her words ring hollow. They have little effect because an acquaintance does not know you well enough to be genuinely concerned.

Conversely, some people may feel compassion but cannot move past their own pain or problems to offer comfort to others. They listen to others' difficulties and immediately launch into an explanation of how their suffering is much greater.

You and I serve as vessels of God's compassion. Self-centeredness blocks the flow of God's comfort to those around us in need of it. When we take our eyes off of our own issues to help those who are hurting, it brings our situation into perspective. Comfort often takes the form of a listening ear, soothing words, hugs, and a handkerchief offered to tear-stained cheeks.

8. Take a moment to recall an act of compassion you have received that stands out in your memory. How did it cause you to feel?

_____

_____

9. Did it change how you felt about the person who offered it?

_____

_____

If our hearts overflow with compassion over the hurts of others, just think of how much our heavenly Father's heart is filled to overflowing with compassion and love for His beloved children.

Deuteronomy 4:31 tells us, "The LORD your God is a merciful God." God's amazing compassion is backed by action. He loves us too much to allow us to perish in our sin. In fullness of compassion, He provided His Son as the atoning sacrifice.

10. What attributes of God are mentioned in Exodus 34:6?

_____

_____

Compassion, grace, love, and faithfulness merely scratch the surface of God's goodness.

Paul showed compassion on God's people in Corinth because of deep love. Jesus had died for them, too, so Paul esteemed them by speaking the truth in love. But rather than beating them over the heads with facts, he used compassion and love to convey God's truths.

In the days following the fire, Jennie and her daughters received an avalanche of compassion—phone calls, text messages, gift cards, furniture, and more. Each day brought new and amazing blessings, and they still marvel over each one.

Today, Jennie and her daughters have a new home, and they work together to build their future as a family. They share a special bond that formed when God's refining fire touched their lives. Each day, they look for and discuss the amazing ways Jesus blesses them *that day*. Jennie never wants to take God's provision and comfort for granted. They talk about how to pay that love and compassion forward.

With the comfort of Jesus working through their hands and the love of God speaking through their lips, they jump at the opportunities to help others facing difficult times.

Blessed be the Father of mercies.

Day 2

Adopted in Love

Long before the fire consumed Jennie's home, a different fire consumed her heart. Although not married, she longed to offer a stable home to children.

As a teacher, Jennie had seen many children exhibit serious behavioral problems, relational difficulties, or poor performance in school because they did not have a stable home life. So she began to pray about how she could help. God soon put the desire in her heart to adopt. But not to adopt just any children—God prompted her to adopt older girls who had been trapped in the foster system for years. More-difficult, troubled young girls, not moldable, newborn babies.

These girls would have behavioral issues. Abandonment scars. Destructive habits. *Fear of trust.* Jennie knew God was calling her to show compassion, demonstrate unconditional love, and provide a good home for these girls while giving them a chance at a normal life. Trusting the Father of mercies, she moved forward toward His calling for her, trusting Him to fill in the gaps.

1. Have you ever followed through on a calling from God when you couldn't see the end result? What happened?

_____

_____

2. What did God show you in the process?

_____

_____

Adoption brings a sense of belonging. A family to call your own brings an enormous sense of comfort.

3. What does Ephesians 1:5 say about our adoption by God?

_____

_____

God *predestined* us, which means He intended to adopt us from the very beginning of the world. Before you were born, He chose you to live with Him in eternity. God has adopted us as sons and daughters, along with all that implies, through baptismal water and the power of His Word.

4. Since we have been adopted, what titles does God bestow on us?

Ephesians 3:6

_____

Romans 8:16

_____

1 John 3:2

_____

Just as Hannah is part of Jennie's family, you and I are part of God's forever family through adoption. That truth fosters unending comfort from the inside out. As God's people, we are not just randomly gathered as a generic flock. We have undergone spiritual adoption into the family of God.

5. What do the following verses tell us about our adoption?

John 1:12–13

_____

Romans 8:15–17

_____

2 Corinthians 6:18

_____

Galatians 4:5–6

_____

Hannah and Ashley rarely experienced compassion or comfort before Jennie adopted them. Both arrived on her doorstep, a few years apart, jaded by years of being shuffled through the foster care system. They were concerned only about their own interests, fiercely guarding what was theirs. They shared belongings through gritted teeth, following fierce arguments. They marked out their territory and defended it.

Over time, as Jennie faithfully took them to church, God began softening and mending their hearts. Hannah said:

> Before the fire, I didn't have the relationship with Jesus that I do now. I constantly kept track of what I gave to be sure I received in return. I never felt contentment. I saw the awesome relationship my mom had with Jesus, and I wasn't acting like that. I see now that God used the fire to get my attention. Now I can see more and more what I can do for others instead of myself. I don't count my life by the man I'm going to marry or the number of children I want to have. It's about who I can help today.

Trials by fire, both physical and spiritual, tend to change us from the inside out. Fires that change more than our address.

Refining fire that changes the landscape of our hearts and ushers in new life.

But God, the Father of all mercies, pours comfort like salve on the wounds. Just think about the apostle Paul. Formerly known as Saul, he committed horrendous crimes against Christians.

6. According to the following verses, what did his life look like before Jesus met him on the road to Damascus?

Acts 8:1–3

Acts 9:1–5

We may tend to believe that someone like Saul does not deserve the comfort of the Father of mercies. Yet, although you and I likely have never committed such crimes, aren't we just as guilty?

Guilty of judging.

Persecuting by gossip.

In the fullness of compassion, Jesus voluntarily died so we could live.

Today, Hannah is a well-adjusted, beautiful, 14-year-old piano player. Ashley is a lovely, dynamic, 13-year-old student. They both love Jesus and know that He saved them from a very difficult foster life.

They have experienced adoption. So can you.

God, our Father of mercies, offers us ultimate comfort through the transformative, refining fires in our lives. Adoption into God's family provides an eternal home for all who surrender to Jesus as Lord.

Comfort without end.

Blessed be the Father of mercies.

Day 3

WHEN COMFORT
SHOWS UP

"Christianity is not a religion of comfort—at least not at first." C. S. Lewis

Comfort arrived in trucks carrying seven beds. Some new. Some antique.

All precious.

Jennie and her two daughters needed only three, so the abundance touched her heart. Their old beds were long gone, consumed by fire, along with everything else.

When emergency teams finally allowed residents to return home, Jennie recalled the heartbreaking scene. Blackened stumps littered the charred ground where her home once stood. The smell of burnt dreams assaulted her senses. Ash piles formed stagnant lines of memories where laughter once danced.

What now, Lord?

After the fire, Jennie and the girls found unexpected comfort in one very simple thing—wearing their own clothes. Not new ones, but those they had packed before the fire took everything else. Although they didn't have a home of their own for two weeks, simply putting on familiar clothes each day boosted Jennie's confidence and ability to handle each day's challenges. It was the personal touch she needed to stay grounded, focused, and walking through each day following the fire.

Jennie saw her home's ashes, but she received basic comfort from a Savior who restores. She said:

> Comfort from God means absolute trust and reliance. It's never questioning that He will provide for me and my daughters' needs. Even something as simple as familiar clothes.

1. Can you recall a time when you felt God's comfort through something very simple? Describe it here.

_____

_____

2. How did that make you feel?

_____

_____

When God breathes simple comfort into our suffocating circumstances, we find ourselves thankful for His wonderful mercies. In the Old Testament account of Job, everything he held dear was taken from him, but not because he transgressed against God. God knew that when the going got tough, the tough leaned on God. God knew Job's integrity and character.

3. What did Job lose according to Job 1:13–19?

_____

_____

4. Have you ever sustained such staggering losses in your life?

_____

_____

5. How did you handle it?

_____

_____

6. Did you feel God's comfort?

_____

_____

Although Job could have chosen anger and bitterness, he chose something infinitely better: *worship.*

7. Immediately after hearing about the horrible tragedies, what was Job's reaction according to Job 1:20–21?

_____

_____

8. What was your initial reaction when you experienced loss?

_____

_____

I saw firsthand how Jennie responded like Job. Although she expressed sadness at her loss, she turned *toward* God, not away from Him. She leaned toward Him. She displayed grace when she could have chosen differently.

The apostle Paul observed that the people of Corinth lost something much more valuable than their possessions. In striving to be prosperous, they forgot about the One who blessed them in the first place. As Paul wrote in his letters to the Corinthians, he was well aware that the people sought comfort in readily available worldly pleasures.

Located on the isthmus that connected the Peloponnesus (the southwestern corner of Greece) to the rest of Greece, Corinth was a thriving port city. The well-trafficked, diverse population of about 600,000 prospered as the commercial and political capital of Achaia. The bustling commercial endeavors did not revolve around religious activity or worship.

The people of Corinth needed to know about a Savior who restores.

Throughout 1 Corinthians, Paul addressed prevalent issues of cultural diversity in the Church, immorality, superstitions, philosophical beliefs, and false doctrines. He used logic, hyperbole, rhetorical questions, and contrasts to teach about the power of the cross (1 Corinthians 1:26–2:5), the transforming work of the Spirit of God (1 Corinthians 2:6–3:4), conflict resolution (1 Corinthians 6:1–11), marriage and relationships (1 Corinthians 7), idols and eating (1 Corinthians 8:1–11:1), worship (1 Corinthians 11:2–14:40), and love (1 Corinthians 13–14).

As Paul penned 2 Corinthians, he began by telling the people about the God of all comfort (2 Corinthians 1:3). Paul loved the people so much that he did not want them to lose heart in their struggles to follow Christ.

So he reminded them about a Savior who comforts.

Write out **2 Corinthians 1:3–7:**

_____

_____

_____

_____

9. What do those words mean to you today?

_____

_____

When we endure difficult seasons, Paul's words remind us to take heart. Comfort shows up when we look to God.

10. What words of comfort do you notice in 2 Corinthians 3:16–18?

_____

_____

Although pain and loss hurt for a time, they are light and momentary compared to the eternal glory God is working in us.

The wildfire that destroyed Jennie's home certainly didn't seem light and momentary. But now that several months have passed, she looks around in wonder at God's abundant provision. In His matchless wisdom, God surrounded Jennie and the girls with many people who had been through the exact same disaster. They were able to offer Jennie much-needed, helpful advice from the path of experience.

The beauty God resurrected like a phoenix from the ashes has far surpassed her wildest dreams. She and her girls share stronger bonds of faith and trust.

In one another.

In God.

Forged by His refining fire. Painful, yet wondrous. Displayed in minute, astonishing detail.

Blessed is the Father of mercies.

Day 4

Losers Are the Best Givers

The morning sun shone bright and warm. The birds sang with gusto as they scrounged for their morning meal. The still beauty of the park showed no signs of the terrible wildfire that consumed Jennie's house the day before.

She pulled into the peaceful park, turned off the minivan's ignition, and turned to her two daughters. And together they cried. Leaning against one another.

Leaning on Jesus.

They huddled close to grieve their tremendous loss. Everything had happened so fast after the fire. They just needed time to breathe. Time to honestly come to grips with their devastating loss.

1. Can you think of a time when you needed to do the same thing?

_____

_____

2. Did you take the time to properly grieve before moving on too fast?

_____

_____

This deep grieving wasn't new for Hannah or Ashley. Living in foster homes for years, they were used to shuffling from house to house, seeing more of life than many of us would care to. Yet, in their young minds, they hoped to eventually end up back home with their birth mother and biological families.

Surely their moms would want them. Surely their families would come looking for them.

But when Jennie adopted them, they eventually realized that their biological families were no longer a part of their lives. As each arrived at that devastating conclusion, they had to take time to mourn that overwhelming loss.

The adoption agency warned Jennie that it takes a couple of years for a foster child to reach that upsetting conclusion. Jennie remembers those very hard, demoralizing days.

Jennie and the girls understand loss.

3. If you have experienced shocking loss, how did you process your grief and receive comfort?

_____

_____

Sometimes, those who lose much tend to give much. When you have to start from scratch, you realize the difference between want and need. Their experience with the fire went a long way in helping Jennie's family understand the difference and the importance of giving back to others in need. The girls don't fight over material possessions anymore or argue over who owns what.

It taught them to hold the stuff of this world loosely.

Surviving hard times also allows us to empathize with others, enter into their pain, and understand on a deeper level how to offer specific comfort.

4. What does the apostle Paul say about loss in Philippians 3:7–9?

_____

_____

5. What strikes you most about those verses? Why?

_____

_____

Paul went through terrible pain and loss during his ministry; yet he continued to keep his eyes focused on God and give everything he had for the sake of the Gospel. Loss made Paul a better giver.

We tend to associate loss with a person or objects. Yet sometimes we lose much more valuable, intangible things. Perhaps you have lost faith, trust, hope, love, or innocence. When we lose tangible or intangible things, it provides an opportunity to evaluate the importance (or not) of what we lost. If we consider it valuable, we come to a clearer understanding of its worth when we offer it to others. As it was with Paul, loss makes us better givers too.

If you have experienced a loss of trust, perhaps you give better in the integrity department. You set a high bar for yourself to spare others enduring such pain from you. Let's look at some examples in Scripture by recording what they lost and gave.

6. What was lost? What was given?

Joseph
Genesis 37:12–24   **Genesis 45:1–14**

_____   _____

Jesus
Matthew 27:45–50   **John 11:25**

_____   _____

Although Joseph lost trust in his brothers, God worked forgiveness in him and allowed Joseph to give love and provision to his brothers.

Jesus lost His life to give us everlasting life.

7. How have your loss experiences allowed you to be a better giver? Or have they?

_____

_____

I don't know about you, but I'm much more comfortable giving than receiving. I love doing for others and seeing the comfort and joy it brings to them. Yet sometimes when I need that from others, I shy away from seeking it.

There is no shame in needing.

God created us to live together in relationship to provide strength when we are weak, love when we feel unlovable, and comfort when we're most uncomfortable.

8. God provides comfort even when we choose to lick our wounds in private. How do you see that in Psalm 23:4?

_____

_____

Sometimes, God gifts us with comforters who have walked our valleys of pain. In Jennie's case, a family volunteering at the fire donation center had lost their home to fire several months earlier. That family knew what such a loss cost emotionally, spiritually, physically, and financially, so they came to offer comfort and help to those who lost everything in the wildfires.

One particular lady homeschooled her children, which allowed her to volunteer at the donation center every day. Jennie was able to tell that lady exactly what she needed, and that wonderful lady kept a close eye on incoming donations and called Jennie if something came in that they specifically needed.

9. Have you been blessed with a comforter who walked a similar painful road to yours?

_____

_____

10. How did that change your perspective about passing that blessing forward?

_____

_____

When you and I suffer loss, we have a choice. We can choose to get angry, lash out, withdraw, and turn bitter. Or we can allow our losses to turn us into better people, capable of helping others in need.

The Son humbled Himself and counted equality with God as nothing for thirty-three years to give us life.

Blessed be the Father of mercies.

Day 5

Embracing Contentment

In the days after Jennie lost her home to the Texas wildfires, one phrase became her mantra: *"If all we have today is our salvation, it's enough. That's all we need."* Some days were so hard that she found herself saying it several times a day to Hannah and Ashley. But mainly to herself.

1. Would you be able to say that statement with conviction when faced with such a loss? Why or why not?

_____

_____

As a teacher and single mom, Jennie lives simply. Budgeting, clipping coupons, and advanced planning for purchasing large-ticket items are normal, everyday habits. She and the girls find great joy in handcrafting gifts and things to make their house a home. Hannah said:

> The fire is a day I'll always remember, but it's also the day that made me realize everything I take for granted. You feel like everything's gone. But I realized that I did all the things I did every day with what I had. I can still do what I need to do every day without the things I no longer have.

A very bright, astute young lady, don't you think? In the two weeks after the fire, when all they owned fit in their minivan, Jennie and her daughters talked at length about living in contentment. They discussed how contentment with material things God provides leads to a greater understanding of being content in every circumstance spiritually.

2. What do you consider to be the basic necessities in your life?

_____

_____

3. How would you define contentment?

_____

_____

You and I live and operate in a culture that believes enough is never enough. Long lines to buy the hottest new item cause deadly stampedes during holiday sales. Plastic surgeons buy airtime to convince people that their life depends on having a perfect body. The perfect teeth. A flawless tan.

We play the stock market. Pull the slot machines. Pay for lottery tickets. Peruse store racks. And somewhere deep down, we've bought the lie that if we don't own the latest gadget, drive the newest car, or own the most lavish home, we're irrelevant. We think we need it all.

The line between needs and wants becomes invisible. Yet loss awakens awareness. It whittles our perspective down to the basics.

4. What does the apostle Paul say about contentment?

2 Corinthians 9:8

_____

2 Corinthians 12:10

_____

Philippians 4:11–12

_____

God instructs us to seek and find contentment in Him alone. He provides for our every need. If we don't have certain material possessions or extra money today, we don't need it today. If we did, God would have given it to us.

The word *content* originates from the Latin *contentus,* that is, "having restrained desires." *Restrained* is not the first word that comes to mind when I think of our culture today.

Spiritual rest and soul quietness die in the midst of constant striving. Whether our striving plays out in climbing the corporate ladder or volunteering to the point of exhaustion simply for recognition, contentment comes when we understand that God has given us everything we need for today. And He will do the same for tomorrow. And the day after that, and so on.

5. What do these verses teach us about contentment?

Hebrews 13:5–6

1 Timothy 6:6–10

You and I are not born with the gift of contentment. Just ask a two-year old who can't have the toy she wants. Contentment is learned, not inherited. Galatians 5:22–23 lists the fruit of the Spirit, yet contentment does not make the list. Our self-centered, sinful nature places our wants on the same level as our needs. And our society fuels that greatly.

Hard lessons learned through experience teach us. Before becoming a Christian twenty years ago, my late teenage/early adult years were filled with self-imposed financial hardship. I misused credit cards and drove myself deep into debt. As if that wasn't enough, I knowingly floated bad checks to get cash back on grocery purchases just to be able to pay the rent due to my out of control spending habits.

Discontentment paints an ugly picture.

The more possessions we acquire, the more time, energy, and resources we deploy to protect them. We put security fences around our excess. Subscribe to home-warning systems to scare off potential thieves. Install hidden cameras to monitor our stuff.

Proverbs 15:16 shines the light of truth regarding contentment. Write out this verse.

_____

_____

_____

Contentment rises from an inward disposition originating in humility that exercises intelligent consideration of God's blessings, the greatness of His promises, and our own unworthiness as we rely on the Gospel for rest and peace.

Let me offer a startling picture of our culture's level of discontentment. As of May 2011, the total U.S. consumer debt topped $2.43 trillion. More than 609 million credit cards are held by U.S. consumers, or an average of nine cards per person. The average household carries $15,799 in credit card debt. (Source: Federal Reserve's G.19 report on consumer credit, released July 2011)

Contentment has been replaced by credit cards.

6. What are you striving for in this season of life?

_____

_____

7. Does _content_ describe your heart?

_____

_____

Jennie and the girls learned that all they need is home, food, clothing, and each other. Hannah said:

Coming from the foster system, it's not the things that matter the most, it's the people who stick with you through the toughest times and grow together.

The fire enabled them to realize they could still serve God with what they had now just as much as with what they had had before—only in different ways. Losing material possessions simply provided an opportunity to find new avenues in which to serve God and help others.

God, in His infinite wisdom, sometimes removes what we think we need to reveal what we truly need.

Blessed be the Father of mercies.

Lesson 1
SMALL-GROUP DISCUSSION

Jennie and her daughters suffered a devastating loss when their home was consumed by raging wildfires. The road back to normal life taught them many lessons along the way.

1. If you have suffered a similar loss, did you rely on God's comfort and provision?

_____

_____

2. What about a time when you were offered comfort by both a loved one who knows you well and a mere acquaintance? From which one were you more open to receiving comfort? Why?

_____

_____

3. If you have been adopted or gone through the adoption process like Jennie has, how has it helped you understand our adoption by God? (See John 1:12–13; Romans 8:15–17)

_____

_____

4. Often, God provides comfort through something very simple. How have you seen that in your life? How did that make you feel?

_____

_____

5. Did your loss experiences make you a better giver? If so, how?

_____

_____

6. Read Philippians 4:11–12. How you do define contentment? Do you believe you abide in contentment? Why or why not?

_____

_____

GOD OUR COMFORTER

The Gift of Affliction

"Blessed be the God of all comfort, who comforts us in all our affliction."
2 Corinthians 1:3–4

Linda loved to travel with her family. Whether the trip took them across town or halfway around the world, she delighted in experiencing life to the fullest with her husband and four children.

I met Linda fifteen years ago when we ended up together on our church's women's retreat planning team. Her love for Jesus flowed through everything she did. She carefully considered and executed countless details to ensure that each woman who attended felt welcomed and loved.

It was easy to love Linda, and we became close friends as the years went by. She was a prayer warrior and an amazing woman of faith. I considered it a great privilege to be her friend.

In 2011, she joined me on a Christian fellowship cruise where I had been invited to teach Bible studies and lead worship onboard. She brought her mom, her mom's best friend, and her mother-in-law to experience Jesus in a fresh new way on the high seas, surrounded by God's stunning creation.

She committed to the cruise because her latest bout of cancer had subsided. One sunny afternoon, on the ship's topmost deck, we reclined side by side on chaise lounges, talking about life. It was a cherished conversation because lack of time did not hurry our words or interrupt deep thoughts.

As the sun warmed our skin and the salt air soothed our senses, she marveled at the strong love that God continued to nurture between her and her husband. She thanked God for molding their children into such fine young adults. Then she said one startling, life-changing statement:

"I'm thankful for the gift of cancer."

Stunned, I turned my head to see her face. She sat up, looked me in the eye, and with an unshakeable peace, described how the gift of cancer allowed her to love freely. Forgive easily. Appreciate every moment fully.

Cancer had enabled her to live bravely. She shared the Gospel without fear, spoke hope to the hopeless, and talked honestly with loved ones to mend relationships long ago relegated to the sidelines.

Linda's unforgettable words reverberated through my heart as I accepted her husband's invitation to share several Scripture passages at her funeral not long ago. Brain cancer had claimed her life, but with great compassion, she wanted to make sure that everyone who attended her funeral knew that the casket was not the end of her story. Or theirs.

It was just the beginning.

She chose Bible verses that pointed to a love beyond the grave. A Savior who took nails in His hands and feet to ensure that nails in our coffin did not eternally separate us from Him.

Linda thanked God for her cancer because it allowed her to live real. She could have been self-centered, bitter, and angry. But we would have missed being encouraged by her faith that persevered even in the midst of terrible physical suffering.

In the lives of those who knew her, and now all those reading this study, I pray that the lessons she learned and shared through her gift of cancer make a lasting impact.

Day 1

THE GIFT OF CANCER

"Affliction is a treasure, and scarce any man hath enough of it." John Donne

Many people do not see cancer as a gift. They see it as an unfair turn in the game of life. An unwarranted struggle. A death sentence.

Destructive.

Invasive.

When Linda called her cancer a gift, it drastically changed how I viewed serious illness. My dad died from cancer nine years ago, and I certainly didn't call it a gift in his case. Although I can't speak for my dad, I never heard him call it that either.

How do you reach the point of calling cancer a gift?

Throughout Scripture, we see many people suffering from leprosy, lameness, and blindness, to name a few afflictions. We don't see them thanking God for their diseases. Rarely do we see them relying on God to comfort them.

The key is thanking God despite your circumstances, not for the circumstance itself.

1. Have you ever battled a life-threatening disease?

_____

2. How did you handle it?

_____

_____

3. Looking back, is there anything you would handle differently?

_____

_____

If you said yes to that last question, I would venture a guess that your response revolves around people. Things said or not said. Kindnesses received and offered. A broader perspective given of the fragility of life and the precious little time we have here.

Take a look at Job's illnesses. He did not know if he would survive them. All he knew was that he was suffering.

4. In the following passages, how do you see Job handling his afflictions?

Job 2:7–10

_____

Job 3:24–26

_____

Job 6:8–10

_____

Job 7:20–21

_____

Job despaired over his illness and hurt in his suffering. He cried out to God for understanding. Those are normal reactions to severe illnesses. He even wanted God to end his life so he wouldn't have to suffer anymore. Yet Job never sinned against God as he suffered.

5. Although he complained and cried out, Job never crossed that line.*
And at the end of his illness, how did he respond to God?

Job 40:3–5

_____

Job 42:1–6

_____

Job didn't understand the reason for his suffering, and God never told him. He simply accepted that God knew what He was doing. Job realized that God wasn't causing suffering just to watch him suffer.

There was a greater purpose that he could not fully see.

When I spoke with Linda's husband, Ray, a few months after her passing, he said that Linda accepted her cancer diagnosis as a platform from which to shine the spotlight on God. Even though she had difficult days, she never wanted to hide from the world or sit on her own pile of ashes, metaphorically speaking.

She realized there was a greater purpose she could not fully see.

Even though Ray sometimes wanted to withdraw, to a certain extent, out of sheer exhaustion from answering everyone's questions about how Linda was doing, he said Linda never wanted to be a hermit. In many instances, Linda offered comfort to others about her own condition because they were heartbroken over her suffering.

6. How do the following verses offer comfort?

Psalm 46:1–2

_____

Psalm 48:14

_____

God is our Comforter and our strength. When I hear the word *cancer* now, two thoughts simultaneously race through my brain: suffering and opportunity. The condition of cancer causes us to suffer a great deal—emotionally, physically, and spiritually. But it also creates an opportunity.

To live better.

Love much.

Die well.

I saw Linda accomplish all three of those tasks in the last three years of her life. She took no friendship or kindness for granted. She loved fiercely through encouragement, hugs, and prayer. And she died well. When I say that, I mean that she taught me how to die with grace. And probably a whole lot of other people too.

She didn't kick or scream about her diagnosis being unfair. She made her relationship with God and other people the main priorities.

She focused on life in the midst of death.

Linda's love so clearly reflected Jesus' compassion for the lost and hurting.

7. As you write out the following life-giving verses, reflect and listen to God's comforting compassion:

Matthew 14:14

Matthew 20:34

Mark 6:34

Our Savior's compassion sets an example for all of us. Did you notice that Jesus not only had compassion for their physical needs, but their spiritual needs as well? Mark 6:34 showed us Jesus tending to their souls. He saw their spiritual hunger, so He began to teach.

Are you able to thank God despite your difficulties? He doesn't ask us to be thankful for our hardships. He asks us to be thankful through them. The apostle Paul translated that truth in Philippians 3:7–11:

> But whatever gain I had, I counted as loss for the sake of Christ. Indeed, I consider everything as loss because of the surpassing worth of knowing Christ Jesus my Lord. For His sake I have suffered the loss of all things and count them as rubbish, in order that I may gain Christ and be found in Him, not having a righteousness of my own that comes from the law, but that which through faith in Christ, the righteousness from God that depends on faith—that I may know Him and the power of His resurrection, and may share His sufferings, becoming like Him in His death, that by any means possible I may attain the resurrection from the dead.

If you or a loved one are struggling with a debilitating or life-threatening circumstance, take this opportunity to lay down this book and kneel before God. Whether through clenched teeth or sorrow-filled tears, tell Him exactly what you're feeling today. Ask Him to strengthen you for the journey ahead, even if you can't see the end of it yet.

Then be still before Him to receive His comfort.

Ask Him to show you how you can use that circumstance to shine His light through you to those around you.

Ask Him to grant you a thankful heart.

Not for your hardship, but for His loving guidance through it.

Day 2

LOVE BEYOND THE GRAVE

Understanding the limited time left with her family motivated Linda to provide a way to ensure her husband and children would continue to travel together after she was gone—that despite busy schedules, they would still make time for one another.

At Linda's request, she was cremated and her ashes divided among four urns. Over the next two years, her family will travel together to bury her remains in four places that are special to them. The last urn will be laid to rest in our church's cemetery. As Linda's family travels to those four places together, her love will go with them.

God's love for you goes with you wherever you go as well. He loves you with an everlasting love. A love that outlasts the grave.

1. What do these verses reveal about God's amazing love for you?

Romans 5:8

_____

Galatians 2:20

_____

Jeremiah 31:3

_____

John 3:16

_____

Often with great love comes great pain.

Jesus suffered greatly.

The greater the love, the more concentrated the pain. The more invested our hearts, the more painful the hurt.

2. Have you ever caused a loved one pain, physical or otherwise? How did you feel?

We grieve when we cause loved ones' pain and suffering. We think about them constantly, communicate with them often, and need assurance that they are going to be all right.

Do we treat Jesus the same way? He experienced the cruelest form of torture so we would be free from sin and have the amazing opportunity to have a relationship with Him throughout eternity.

3. How do you see that truth in the following verses?

Hebrews 10:1–14

Isaiah 53:3–5

Jesus was crucified. He was wounded for our transgressions.

Not His.

The One who loves us infinitely beyond our understanding was wounded. Knowing that is bad enough. But we are not just innocent bystanders to the horrific event of Jesus' crucifixion. He was wounded wholly and specifically because of us.

Jesus was the One-for-all sacrifice that would guarantee eternal life to all who believe that He died, rose from the grave, and has gone to prepare a place for us in heaven.

4. What comfort do you find in knowing He's getting your heavenly dwelling ready?

_____

_____

He is preparing a place for us with Him. Jesus endured unbelievable suffering and soul-saving sacrifice as He willingly carried out the greatest act of love ever demonstrated.

Because of His sacrifice, we, too, find love beyond the grave.

When we think of cancer and graves, we automatically think of death. Yet the end of John 3:16 states that we "should not perish but have eternal life." God has provided the means for us to be reconciled with Him. We place our trust in His promises.

Trust and faith go hand in hand. When we trust God and take Him at His Word, we come to Him in faith to receive His reconciliation and abundant life.

God loves you.

He desires for you to experience His love beyond the grave.

And tell others about it in the meantime.

Day 3

AFFLICTED IN LOVE

"Those who dive in the sea of affliction bring up rare pearls."
Charles Spurgeon

When we see loved ones suffer, we often wonder why. As I saw the effects of cancer ravage Linda's body, her affliction hurt my heart because I loved her a great deal.

We might even ask God why people need to suffer—especially if they shine God's light and love brightly. Why would He choose to put that light out?

As we break and crack under affliction, God's glory and grace shine through those breaks. We see His beauty through the cracks of suffering.

Write out this week's verse from the front of this chapter (2 Corinthians 1:3–4):

_____

_____

God promises to comfort us in all our affliction. You and I will experience affliction. Period. Throughout Scripture, we see God's people experiencing suffering and affliction. Those whom God used in mighty ways also suffered in mighty ways. "Affliction" can refer to both outward circumstances and inward states of mind.

1. Identify the inward or outward affliction you see in the following verses:

2 Corinthians 2:4

_____

2 Corinthians 7:4–5

---

2 Corinthians 4:17

---

2 Corinthians 6:4

---

2 Corinthians 8:2

You and I experience suffering on many levels so that God can use us to comfort others on many levels.

When it comes to suffering, consider Mary. As the story unfolds in Luke 1, Gabriel appeared to Mary with the announcement that she, one highly favored, had been chosen to be the mother of God's Son.

As Mary likely faced ridicule (and worse) once she shared the news that she was a pregnant virgin, I wonder if she felt highly favored. As Mary made a seventy-mile journey, on foot or on donkey-back, at the very end of her pregnancy, I wonder if she thought that God could have arranged the census for a later date.

As Joseph and Mary arrived in Bethlehem only to discover no room in the inn, I wonder if it crossed her mind that God could have arranged room reservations for His Son.

When the time came for Mary to give birth, Luke's Gospel makes no mention of a midwife or even another mom present to help her with that process. Only Joseph.

Later, when Joseph and Mary fled to Egypt to escape Herod, I wonder if Mary cried out to God when she learned about the death of all those children age 2 and under.

She watched her Son live a perfect life, only to watch Him die a criminal's death, nailed to our cross of shame.

I just wonder what Mary wondered.

Mary suffered greatly, yet God never explained everything to her. In the midst of it all, Mary trusted. She may have wondered why she suffered, but she still walked in obedient faith.

2. Following Gabriel's amazing announcement, what were Mary's words of faithful trust in Luke 1:38?

_____

_____

3. When you face uncertain times that prove uncomfortable, how do you typically respond?

_____

_____

God never allows pain just to watch us suffer. He promises in Isaiah 61 to bind up the brokenhearted and comfort all who mourn. As we suffer under trials, God strengthens us for even greater tests of faith. Through trials, God builds in us His strength to endure the race He's marked out for us. Yet, through the trials, He promises comfort.

4. What do these verses reveal to you about God, the giver of comfort?

Psalm 86:17

_____

Isaiah 12:1

_____

Isaiah 51:3

_____

Isaiah 66:13

God's healing love is our unfailing comfort. Our love can change people. *But God's love saves them.*

When Paul wrote 2 Corinthians, he was experiencing affliction and anguish because of his love for the believers in Corinth. Paul observed that though he and his fellow believers were afflicted in every way, perplexed, persecuted, and struck down, they relied on God to see them through (2 Corinthians 4:7–12). Paul also records many difficulties he and those with him endured.

5. What did these include according to the following verses?

2 Corinthians 6:4–5

2 Corinthians 11:23–28

The Pauline entourage endured suffering in Asia as well as Macedonia, where they were "afflicted at every turn—fighting without and fear within" (2 Corinthians 7:5). Paul himself was afflicted with a "thorn . . . in the flesh" to keep him humble. Because of his thorn, Paul recognized that our afflictions have divine purposes. He realized it was better not to look at the things of this life because they will not last.

6. According to 2 Corinthians 4:17–18, on what do we need to focus?

7. As we focus on the glory of God, His angels, and heaven, it puts our suffering in perspective. When we are weak in our suffering, what does God promise in 2 Corinthians 12:9–10?

_____

_____

In the midst of these afflictions, it is God who "comforts the downcast" (2 Corinthians 7:6). Since God ultimately delivered Paul from his affliction, he trusted that God would deliver him again (1:10).

When our loves ones suffer, we suffer along with them. I watched Linda's husband, Ray, and their four children suffer right along with Linda because of their great love for her. They didn't understand why she had to be afflicted in such a way, yet they used her trial of cancer as a platform to share the love of Christ. And through that, they received comfort.

From family and friends.

And from God Himself.

Day 4

CAREGIVERS AS GOD'S COMFORTERS

For the three years that Linda battled cancer, her husband, Ray, cared for her. He took her to doctor visits and chemotherapy sessions, held her when she needed to be comforted, made arrangements for her care when he needed be away for work, and so much more.

Ray was a wonderful caregiver for his wife, and his understanding about comfort provides us with invaluable insights.

1. Have you ever taken care of a seriously ill loved one?

_____

2. What did that entail for you?

_____

_____

3. How did it make you feel?

_____

_____

Caring for a sick loved one hits us on many levels, especially if that person is a spouse, parent, or child. Caregivers come alongside to offer comfort despite their own grief over their loved one's illness.

In 2 Corinthians 1:4, the apostle Paul states that God "comforts us in all our affliction." Understanding the precise definition of the particular word *comfort* brings the caregiver role into sharp focus. The Greek word for *comfort (parakletos)* in that part of 2 Corinthians 1:4 refers to one who is called to our side. It denotes one who acts on someone else's behalf as a mediator, an intercessor, or an encourager.

Think of the role of a caregiver when reading those three roles. Mediator. Intercessor. Encourager.

At one point or another, caregivers serve as each of those things. They mediate between doctors and hospitals to weigh and choose appropriate treatment based on information provided by medical professionals. They intercede on behalf of their sick loved one to God and to others as they seek guidance. And caregivers offer encouragement in countless ways to keep up the spirits of the one for whom they care.

God uses caregivers to pour comfort into those who are sick. But God's comfort for those who are suffering doesn't end at the caregiver level.

4. Who is identified as our *Parakletos,* or Comforter, in the following verses?

John 14:26

_____

John 15:26

_____

The Holy Spirit is called our *Parakletos,* our Comforter, because He works within us to comfort and guide us.

5. Another word for "comforter" is *Advocate.* Who is identified as our Comforter in 1 John 2:1?

_____

In 1 John 2:1, Christ is called a *Paraclete* because He represents people to God—similar to His ministry as High Priest (Hebrews 7:25–28). The two Paracletes, or Comforters, or Advocates—Christ and the Holy Spirit—work together in perfect harmony (Romans 8:26–27, 34).

They work in harmony to bring us comfort.

And the caregivers add the human touch of comfort we need.

Sometimes Linda needed to *be* a caregiver as well. As she battled cancer, loved ones and friends were devastated by her illness. As they cried in their grief over her diagnosis, she wiped their tears and held their hands. She needed comfort, yet it blessed her to comfort others.

But some days it became too much.

Each time a new development occurred with her cancer, Linda almost wanted to keep it to herself to spare her loved ones additional grief. She needed consoling and comfort during those downcast times herself, so some days, she simply couldn't muster the energy, courage, or strength to tell anyone outside her family.

6. When we are downcast or mourning, what does God promise in Matthew 5:4?

_____

_____

Have you ever camped out awhile on this particular verse? "Blessed are those who mourn." During times of suffering, most of us don't feel blessed. However, God indeed blesses us by sending to us His Comforter and wonderful caregivers.

People cannot truly meet our deepest need for comfort, but they can certainly provide the heart salve for a short period. Why just a short period? Because people's mercies run out.

7. Whose mercies are new every morning according to Lamentations 3:22–23?

_____

_____

Only God's mercies are new every morning.

Caregivers can wear out.

During the time of Linda's illness, Ray craved good teaching and in-depth Bible study. Between taking care of Linda and work, he did not have time for serious Bible study on his own. He drank in sermons and Bible class like a camel in the desert to refill and recharge his spiritual reserves.

He became so thankful for those "spiritual reserves." All of those years being involved in church, listening to sermons, being involved in small-group Bible study, and attending Bible class hydrated him for the long haul of battling Linda's cancer alongside her.

Ray drank deep from those spiritual reserve tanks during Linda's illness to remind himself of God's provision, comfort, love, and promises when he needed them most.

God refreshes and refuels the caregivers.

If you find yourself in the role of taking care of a sick loved one, be prepared to offer comfort before you receive it. When difficult news needs to be relayed to family and friends, or when the one who is ill needs comfort, caregivers need focus on God and strength drawn from Him to endure.

Caregivers are precious to God. Indispensible to the sick. And vital conduits of God's comfort and love to the hurting.

As we close today's lesson, take a moment to pray for those caregivers you know. If you currently serve as a caregiver, I hope you will join Isaiah in saying this prayer:

> The Sovereign LORD has given me an instructed tongue
> to know the word that sustains the weary. He wakens me
> morning by morning, wakens my ear to listen like one being
> taught. Isaiah 50:4 (NIV1984)

Day 5

Leaning
on the Comforter

When sudden, unexpected events happen to us, trusting God as our ultimate Comforter means the difference between despair and hope.

As Linda moved into the fight for her life, she found great peace in leaning on the One who breathed life into her. She loved poring through God's Word. Her face lit up when she talked about Scripture and God's love drenching the pages. She nurtured a close relationship with her Savior and received His strength, encouragement, and comfort.

1. Do you find yourself leaning on God during difficult times or trying to fix situations on your own?

_____

_____

We lean on God to provide the comfort He has promised to each and every individual who seeks comfort from Him. I love the King James Version of Psalm 94:19, which says, "In the multitude of my thoughts within me Thy comforts delight my soul."

2. Do you find that God's comfort delights your soul?

_____

_____

Linda delighted in the Lord, His Word, and her relationship with Him. She also delighted in her loving, supportive family and friends. They leaned on one another as well.

Linda, Ray, and their children loved to travel together. As a business owner, Ray worked hard, so Linda organized and planned vacation times so they could refuel as a family.

When Linda became ill, she took time to organize trips for just her and Ray. She nurtured that special relationship with her husband. Ray received great comfort in knowing that Linda cared for him by scheduling rest and relaxation that he would not have taken on his own.

3. Whether married or not, do you take time to recharge and refuel with your family or those close to you?

When we race through life and do not take the time to lean on God for guidance, provision, comfort, and strength, we will run straight into a brick wall of burnout.

You may find yourself in that stage of life right now. Perhaps you're so busy that you cannot even see past today's long to-do list.

And yet God led you to this study.

Today.

I invite you to just stop for a moment and take a deep breath.

4. Slow down your pace long enough to write down these wonderful, comfort-filled verses.

Psalm 119:50

Psalm 119:76

Isaiah 40:1

On our own, we do not have the proper comfort to offer to each other apart from being a vessel of Jesus. Jesus provided great comfort to people while He was here.

Take a moment to read in John 11:32–36 how Jesus comforted Mary and Martha when Lazarus died.

5. What stands out to you in this passage?

_____

_____

Did you notice that "Jesus wept" with the rest of the mourners?

Two simple words. One profound picture.

God in the flesh loved so greatly that when He experienced loss, He grieved. I would suggest that His tears were not only due to the temporary separation from His friend Lazarus, but also due to the compassion He felt for Mary and Martha's pain.

Jesus' friends were hurting, so He hurt as well.

Sometimes the most effective act of compassion is simply to cry with those who cry. No fancy words needed.

Jesus understood hurt. When you and I face difficulties and trials, leaning on Him provides comfort from the inside out. It brings about His peace that surpasses all understanding.

Intentionally lean on Him. Regardless of life's chaos.

He is our refuge, strength, and fortress.

A strong tower when life hurts.

Lesson 2

SMALL-GROUP DISCUSSION

Although cancer is a terrible disease, Linda referred to her cancer as a gift. She said that it allowed her to love freely, forgive easily, live bravely, and appreciate every moment fully.

1. Does her view about cancer change your perspective? Why or why not?

_____

_____

2. In Day 2, we learned that Linda requested her ashes be separated into four urns so her family could continue traveling together over the next few years. If you were to focus on loving beyond the grave, what would that look like in your life?

_____

_____

3. As we suffer through long-term illness, we may ask God why people need to suffer. How would you answer that question if someone were to ask you?

_____

_____

4. If you serve as a caregiver for a loved one, what challenges do you experience? what joys?

_____

_____

5. How have you experienced God refreshing and refueling your spiritual reserves when you are weary?

_____

_____

6. During difficult times, do you lean on the God of all comfort or on something/someone else?

_____

_____

COMFORTED TO COMFORT

Even When You Hurt

"[He comforts us] . . . so that we may be able to comfort those who are in any affliction, with the comfort with which we ourselves are comforted by God." 2 Corinthians 1:4

As Joel took his usual place at the keyboard, he glared at the lyrics printed on the music in front of him.

"Praise to the Lord! O let all that is in me adore Him!" (LSB 790:5)

A muscle tightened in his jaw.

He placed his fingers on the keys and began leading the congregation in worship. He encouraged worshipers to offer praise to a faithful, loving God.

"All that has life and breath, come now with praises before Him!"

He felt like a hypocrite. The last thing he wanted to do was praise God.

Instead of hands raised in surrender, he felt like shaking white-knuckled fists . . . like slinging messy, hurt-filled words rather than expressions of praise.

"Let the amen sound from His people again; Gladly forever adore Him!"

He swallowed the bitterness and forced himself to focus on the task at hand. The sooner the service was over, the better. He spent as little time praising God as possible. He only practiced enough in order to play each song without messing up. Outwardly, he seemed passionate about worshiping God.

Yet anger suffocated his heart.

A wall had been erected by hurt over unexplained loss. Senseless loss. Brick by brick, he put God on the other side of the wall to guard his heart from the pain. He locked that particular hurt away from God and walked away willfully. Hurt and loss caused him to create resolutions.

But it hadn't always been like that.

As far back as Joel could remember, his dad had nurtured him in countless ways. A tenderhearted man, his dad never shrank back from expressing love to him and his two sisters. He delighted in telling them, in every way imaginable, how much both he and God loved them.

His dad spent the majority of his adult life as a missionary in Panama and Brazil. For more than twenty years, he gave up the comforts of living and working in the United States to spread the Gospel in South America. Born and raised in Brazil, Joel served alongside his family with all his heart, soul, mind, and strength to help those in need. He grew up believing that working in God's mission field was a way of life, not a job. Eventually, Joel left South America to attend college in the United States. After his parents gave him good-bye hugs in the airport terminal, he passed through customs and turned back one more time to wave good-bye.

And he saw his dad. Standing there, sobbing uncontrollably, his dad conveyed without words the immeasurable love he felt for his son.

After obtaining his undergraduate degree from Concordia University, Irvine, California, and then spending some time in Chicago, Joel attended Concordia Seminary in St. Louis, Missouri, for two years before receiving his true calling from God. Music. Joel loved music, but not necessarily being in front of a mic. He nurtured a passion to produce music and orchestrate worship services. He left the seminary and headed for Nashville to follow his dream.

Then a phone call changed everything.

After spending all those years as a missionary in Panama, Joel's dad had been diagnosed with brain cancer.

Really, God? He was your hands and feet to an impoverished people in South America for years. Is that how You reward those who devote their whole lives to serving You? Are you kidding me?

Anger settled deep in Joel's heart. Like a three-headed dragon, it roared to the surface, belching fire and smoke, at the slightest provocation.

But God kept knocking on the door of Joel's heart to lead His people in worship.

While in Nashville, Joel received a call to serve as programming director for a brand-new LCMS congregation in Texas. He and his wife moved to Texas, and his anger relocated with them. Joel dug into doing what he loved to do. He was serving God, just like a chip off the old block.

Sadly, the brain cancer advanced rapidly, and Joel's dad passed away before he ever saw Joel leading worship where he'd been called to serve.

The stunning, heartbreaking news sent Joel into a spiritual nosedive. It became harder and harder to keep the anger dragon caged. And the wall Joel built around his heart wasn't keeping the pain out. Brick by brick, the anger dragon repeatedly broke through.

Joel was so tired of fighting it.

He wanted so much to worship God wholeheartedly.

How do you resolve anger with Someone you can't even see?

Day 1

WHEN YOUR HERO DIES

*We can experience joy in adverse circumstances by holding God's benefits in
such esteem that the recognition of them and meditation upon them shall
overcome all sorrow. John Calvin*

It's heartbreaking when your dad dies. But when your hero dies, it
shatters something deeper. After all, a hero can do no wrong. Heroes spark
in us the courage to bravely follow our dreams without pause.

For Joel, his dad and his hero were one and the same. One loss delivered
a double blow.

In today's culture, we tend to think of a movie star or sports figure as a
hero. Sometimes we think of a police officer or firefighter in heroic terms.
Occasionally, we remember a soldier.

**1. By definition, a true hero is noted for noble purposes and feats of
courage. As you look back on your life, have you ever had a hero?**

_____

_____

2. What made that person your hero?

_____

_____

**3. How does 1 Samuel 17:4–7 describe what the Philistines considered a
hero?**

_____

4. What was their response when their hero was killed by David in 1 Samuel 17:50–52?

_____

Our world tends to look at the exterior when determining hero status—big, tall, impressive figures who stand out from the crowd, based on physique or attitude. But a true hero exhibits strength from within. Someone willing to risk his life to save complete strangers.

The disciples thought they had a hero. Jesus didn't look like Goliath, but He performed miracles. Real miracles. He raised the dead. Restored sight to the blind. Turned lame beggars into walking storyboards.

Jesus stood His ground when faced by sneaky church leaders attempting to discredit, trap, and kill Him. He taught radical, irrefutable truths that left religious experts scratching their heads and scrambling for new questions.

Jesus told the disciples that His kingdom would have no end. Thinking Jesus referred to an earthly kingdom, they clamored to know who would sit on His right and His left (Mark 10:35–45).

Jesus fit the hero bill.

But the disciples just didn't get it. The people of Jerusalem shouted with praise as Jesus entered the city triumphantly on Palm Sunday. But mere days later, something went terribly wrong. After the disciples joined Jesus in breaking bread, sharing wine, and making their way to a garden, soldiers appeared and cuffed Him in shackles.

They just didn't get it.

Then, the unthinkable happened. Jesus received a brutal beating and a criminal's death sentence. That wasn't supposed to happen to heroes. When their hero headed up to Calvary, most of the disciples headed for the hills. When Jesus hung on a cross of shame and gasped, "It is finished," the disciples were nowhere in sight. Their hero had died. Their protection was gone.

They just didn't get it.

Jesus' crucifixion shattered the disciples to the core. They wrestled with trying to understand. They struggled to find comfort. From where they stood, God caused their discomfort. What comfort could they pass on to someone else? They needed it desperately themselves.

5. Have you struggled with receiving comfort if you believed God caused your discomfort?

_____

_____

6. What was the result?

_____

_____

When we don't understand a heartbreaking loss or hardship, we may experience anger. Anger can pour deadly poison into our hearts and souls.

7. Take a moment to look up and write out these Scripture passages about anger.

Proverbs 14:29

_____

Proverbs 15:1

_____

Proverbs 15:18

_____

Proverbs 16:32

_____

Proverbs 19:11

_____

These verses point out the spiritual harm anger inflicts—not only on the one experiencing it, but on those around them. Anger is often called a "secondary emotion." We resort to anger in order to protect ourselves from, or cover up, vulnerable feelings.

A primary feeling is what we feel immediately before we feel anger. We almost always feel something first before we get angry.

8. If you have experienced anger recently, think on it for a moment. What sparked your anger?

_____

_____

You might first have felt afraid, attacked, hurt, humiliated, offended, disrespected, forced, trapped, or pressured. If any of these feelings is intense enough, we think of the emotion as anger. But anger represents the tip of an iceberg. Other emotions exist below the waterline where they are not immediately obvious. Identifying those primary emotions holds the key to dealing with anger, and it opens the faucets of comfort.

Anger itself is not wrong. It's what we do or don't do with it that can be wrong. When we work through anger issues, relying on God's help to resolve them, He can then use those experiences to strengthen and grow our faith.

A person struggling with anger finds it difficult to receive comfort. Anger generates a response of lashing out rather than being still and listening—to God or anyone else.

If you have experienced and worked through anger issues and received God's comfort, God has provided a unique opportunity to you. Your experience gives you a deeper understanding and empathy toward others struggling with similar issues.

9. How does 2 Corinthians 1:4 phrase cause and effect process?

_____

_____

As you experience and receive His comfort, God equips you to pour comfort into others dealing with similar pain.

I can relate to Joel's pain and anger. I lost my dad to cancer in 2003, and it broke my heart to watch a vibrant outdoorsman reduced to tube feeding as the cancer ravaged his body. I struggled with his suffering and asked God toxic questions: *Why aren't my prayers making a difference? Don't You hear me? You can heal Dad. Why aren't You?*

As time passed, God answered those questions. I saw how God moved our family closer together during that painful time. We certainly wouldn't have chosen that method, but God did. I simply learned to trust God's wisdom—especially since there was nothing I could do to change my dad's diagnosis. I learned to look to God in hope that He would bring good out of that situation, although I couldn't see it at that time.

God understands. He does not take offense when our hearts bleed ugly questions. Our compassionate, loving God is slow to anger.

10. Write out the following verses that affirm this wonderful truth:

Exodus 34:6

_____

Psalm 86:15

_____

Psalm 145:8–9

_____

God is a compassionate, loving God—even when we are hurting and doubting.

During Dad's last eight days in the hospital, my family and I camped out in the waiting room. About the third day of our vigil, one of Dad's coworkers showed up with a full-blown dinner for our whole family. Through her, God provided a buffet line of comfort. Her compassion shone brightly into our hearts in that small ICU kitchen. She allowed God's comfort to pass through her to us.

As it turns out, that precious lady had lost a loved one to cancer and understood exactly what we needed and what we might be feeling (anger included).

11. What act of compassion you have received particularly stands out in your memory?

_____

_____

Whether your anger originates from hurt over the loss of a loved one or the loss of your hero, God, our ultimate Hero, pours comfort into our parched souls.

Time fosters healing. The disciples' pain was too raw to see the big picture. Although Jesus had told them numerous times how His earthly life would end, they were too busy picturing a different outcome to listen. Jesus' earthly ministry did not turn out as their limited faith envisioned. God's plans far outstrip our meager imaginations.

Joel's dad was his earthly hero. Joel did not envision such a painful ending for his dad. Yet, over time, with the help of godly friends and prayer, Joel worked through his anger and underlying emotions. Joel knows that he will be reunited with his dad in heaven because our ultimate Hero chose to sacrifice His life in the most painful way imaginable.

Joel is a different man today from the man who transferred to the brand-new congregation in Katy, Texas, six years ago. He has surrendered his anger to God and now leads and serves by example. Each week, as he leads worship, his passion and love for the Lord operate as a catalyst for focusing our eyes on our Healer and offering Him our highest praise. God uses the many gifts He's given Joel to lead worship.

Joel understands at the deepest level that God comforts us.

Even when anger gets in the way.

Day 2

MISPLACED EXPECTATIONS

As far back as Joel could remember, his dad's birthday cards topped the best. He would write paragraph after paragraph, telling Joel how much he was loved and how proud he was of the godly man Joel had become.

Looking back, Joel remembered his parents operating as one. The two had become one flesh, and together, they were strong.

But when one parent dies, the other's weaknesses lie exposed. Joel remembers the first birthday card he received from his mom after his dad passed away. Paragraphs of his dad's encouraging, loving words were replaced by: "Love, Mom."

Although he knew that his mom loved him just as much as his dad did, Joel struggled with anger toward his mom. She wasn't picking up the slack in his dad's absence. Joel experienced misplaced expectations. Expecting her to fill in for his dad was unintentional, but since Joel never articulated his expectation, it became a challenge to work through the resulting anger.

1. Have you ever put a misplaced expectation on someone? If so, what was the result?

---

2. Has someone else put a misplaced expectation on you? If so, what was the result?

People are not the only recipients of misplaced expectations. Sometimes we project misplaced expectations on God. For example, when I first became a Christian twenty years ago, I expected my life to start running smoothly. After all, God could fix any problem, right? I unrealistically expected God to remove all of life's struggles and strife. I naively pictured myself waking up each morning like Cinderella, singing with birds and sewing mouse clothes. Well, you get the point.

3. Have you ever put misplaced expectations on God?

_____

4. What were they?

_____

_____

5. What was the result?

_____

_____

Misplaced expectations deliver zero comfort. They leave us feeling let down with no one to blame except the person in the mirror.

Several heroes of faith in the Bible projected misplaced expectations on God. Let's review a few examples.

When God promised to deliver the Israelites from captivity, do you think Moses expected to have to deal with their groaning, complaining, and murmuring for forty years in the desert? Not only that, but imagine Moses' shock when he learned that God wouldn't let him enter the Promised Land, even after such a long, drawn-out ordeal!

6. According to Numbers 20:7–12, why did Moses forfeit his entrance into the Promised Land?

_____

_____

7. What did the Lord allow Moses to do before his death, according to Deuteronomy 34:1–5?

_____

_____

As Moses drank in the sight of the land of milk and honey, the reality of God's great promises to His people hydrated his soul. God provided that unique comfort to Moses out of love.

What about Abraham and Sarah? Abraham was one hundred years old and Sarah was ninety when their son, Isaac, was born. They had blown past retirement age and were elderly, yet they had a baby. Many grandparents today raise their grandchildren, but what about being great-grandparent age and having your first child of your own?

8. What did God promise Abraham according to Genesis 18:10–11?

_____

_____

9. Considering how old she and Abraham were, what was Sarah's response in Genesis 18:12–14?

_____

_____

However, Abraham's misplaced expectations caused him to attempt to speed up God's plan. In Genesis 18, God made the promise to Abraham (who was already an old man) that he would be the father of many nations. Given his age, Abraham likely expected God to deliver soon on His promises. As time wore on—twenty-five years to be precise—Abraham got nervous about his advancing age.

10. According to Genesis 16:1–3, what did Abraham (then known as Abram) do?

_____

_____

The union between Abraham and Hagar still causes religious strife today. Islamic tradition considers Ishmael to be the ancestor of the Arab people, and Muhammad as descended from Ishmael.

Misplaced expectations exact a high price.

In place of misplaced expectations, God's Word provides us with something infinitely better: hope. The biblical definition of _hope_ is "confident expectation."

Not misplaced—_confident_ expectation.

For instance, our hope stands firm because we believe with confident expectation that Jesus is the same "yesterday and today and forever" (Hebrews 13:8).

11. Hope never disappoints. How do you see that truth in Romans 5:5?

_____

_____

The New King James version of Romans 5:5 says, "Now hope does not disappoint, because the love of God has been poured out in our hearts by the Holy Spirit who was given to us."

When you and I experience trials and suffering, misplaced expectation fosters a sense of hopelessness.

12. What does God instruct us about hope in the following passages?

Hebrews 11:1

_____

Romans 15:13

_____

Hope turns our focus like a laser toward the horizon of God's promises revealed in Scripture. Faith receives and takes hold of that vision until it becomes reality.

Now *that's* confident expectation.

13. If you are struggling in a particular friendship or family relationship, evaluate what caused the break in fellowship. Have you embraced some misplaced expectations?

_____

_____

14. If you find yourself distant from God in your times of hardship, have you perhaps projected misplaced expectations on Him?

_____

_____

Joel's misplaced expectations about his mom playing both parental roles caused heartache and disappointment that affected their relationship for a time. Yet Joel kept seeking God for answers. He never gave up. The bond of love that God had created between Joel and his mom provided hope.

15. What does Isaiah 40:31 promise?

_____

_____

Hope is confident expectation. God's promise to comfort us in all our trials allows hope to arise in our hearts.

Faith placed in God alone never leads to misplaced expectations.

Hope makes all the difference.

Day 3

Nurturing with Love

With a family of his own now, Joel loves to nurture his wife and three children. The unconditional love Joel received from his dad laid a solid foundation, enabling him to offer the same to his own children. Joel's wife, Jodie, continually affirms Joel's spiritual leadership in their home. His love for God and his wife provides his family a solid foundation built on Jesus.

Five years after his dad passed away, Jodie put together a photo album of precious times Joel experienced with his father. When Joel discovered that treasured gift on his nightstand, it provided permission and a springboard for remembering his dad often, and the special bond they shared that helped shape Joel into who he is today. Preserving Joel's memories of his dad speaks of Jodie's unconditional love for her husband.

Joel works hard and sacrifices to provide for his family, just like his dad did for them when he was a child in South America. Joel's family sees him sacrifice time and treasure for their sake, and they come to understand how much Joel loves them.

Sacrificial love renders great comfort.

You and I understand that truth in light of Jesus' sacrifice on the cross. If you've been a Christian for any length of time, you know John 3:16 by heart. Take a moment to write it here.

_____

_____

John 3:16 does not contain many words, but it summarizes the very essence of Christ's sacrifice for us and the eternal hope it provides. It starts with God's love and ends with life for absolutely anyone who believes by faith. No exceptions. No barriers. One sacrifice of love, given in love, so that we may remain in His love throughout eternity.

This simple Scripture passage sums up the deepest, inexhaustible truth of our faith. It is the ultimate address of love in the Bible. When our circumstances threaten to drown us in hopelessness, these lifesaving words from God remind us that His love does conquer all. His love embraces all.

His love never forgets where we live.

Martin Luther called this verse "the Bible in miniature." There is no sweeter verse in the whole Bible because it declares loud and clear that God is love. Love goes hand in hand with true comfort. We receive God's love through the Holy Spirit as He works through God's living and active Word, Holy Baptism, the Lord's Supper, and through those precious dear ones He gives us as we travel this life.

God created and knit us together. His love for us far surpasses anything we can conceive. Such unconditional love hydrates us with holy comfort when life blindsides us.

God chooses to love all people, not just the loveable. He loves the difficult. The murderer. The sinner.

You and me.

1. What do these passages say about God's love for us?

Deuteronomy 7:6

_____

Romans 5:8

_____

Ephesians 2:4–5

_____

1 John 3:1

_____

1 John 4:9–10

_____

We see throughout Scripture the preeminence of love. Love represents a vital ingredient in our walk with God and our ability to authentically offer comfort to others in His name.

Love changes lives.

God's love saves them.

Sometimes, however, we opt not to share His love.

Despite all the Valentine's Day cards sentiments to the contrary, love is a choice and an action—not a feeling. We choose to love and comfort our neighbors because God first loved us (1 John 4:19). Holding back His love turns off the faucet of honest comfort.

In our personal relationships with those closest to us, love matures over time by our choices and sacrifices toward one another.

The choice to love or not.

To forgive or not.

Show kindness or not.

God's love for us is so much more than we can imagine. He could choose not to love us—*then* where would we be? He could choose to demand that we keep every law to the letter, or else. He could choose to be cruel and bring down on each of us the wrath we most assuredly deserve.

Instead, He chooses to love.

2. What does 1 John 4:16–21 tell us about God's comforting love?

_____

_____

God's love lives in us. God's love forgives. His mercy endures forever.

Perhaps, as He did for Joel, God has given you the gift of your own family. He has given you the unique opportunity to nurture those closest to you with unconditional love. Comforting, unconditional love poured through you from God Almighty.

3. How will you express your love to your loved ones today?

_____

_____

Day 4

SUFFERING DEFINED

Stillness envelopes the room. A clock ticks faintly in the corner. The kids are upstairs, safely tucked in bed. His wife reads in the other room. The small lamp glows softly, revealing private grief.

Bowed in prayer, Joel voices his painful questions to God. "We had lots of years left; why take Dad so soon? Why make him suffer like that?"

Why?

Perhaps you have asked God that pain-filled question at some point. We have all experienced tragedies or persistent, self-induced spiritual obstacles that have caused suffering in our lives. Rare indeed is the life that is free from all trouble and hardship. The North African bishop and philosopher Augustine once said, "Everywhere a greater joy is preceded by a greater suffering."

Suffering is just a part of life.

God's children were not exempt from hardship and suffering in Old Testament times, and we are not exempt as New Testament believers. The apostle Paul viewed suffering as an inevitable part of the Christian life. He used suffering as an opportunity to lean on God's divine encouragement.

Suffering serves as the training ground for service to the Body of Christ. It equips us so that we can better minister to those who are going through trials and hardships.

Think about it.

You and I normally don't pour out our souls' anguish to a friend who has never suffered. Lack of experience prevents them from understanding at the deepest level.

In 2 Corinthians 1:4, Paul writes that we receive God's comfort, "so that we may be able to comfort those who are in any affliction, with the comfort with which we ourselves are comforted by God." Suffering is not an easy subject because suffering hurts. No matter where or how we suffer, no one really looks forward to enduring it.

Webster defines *suffering* as "physical or mental pain or distress." A definition we would expect. However, the definition of *suffer* stopped me in my tracks. *Suffer* means "to tolerate or endure; to permit or allow." As we apply that profound definition to the pain and hurt we suffer as God's children, the interesting contrast proposes two choices for us:

» We can merely tolerate or endure suffering.

Tolerating and *enduring* carry negative connotations. They bring to mind the look on someone's face when asked to do something he or she clearly has no desire to do. That look conveys a closed mind and unteachable spirit. As Christians, when others ask us to undertake a tedious ministry duty, do we give them the look? Do we give God the look at times, as well?

1. Try to picture the look on the faces in the following passages. What do you see?

The Pharisee in Luke 7:36–39

_____

The disciples in Mark 10:13–16

_____

A negative look speaks volumes—condemnation, judgment, dislike, belittlement. It does not lend comfort or seek to encourage. The look does more harm than good, and it takes much time to repair the damage.

» We can permit or allow suffering.

That definition carries a positive connotation. It denotes a willingness to learn and grow. Jesus provides our most prominent example. Regardless of the many indignities, general rudeness, and outright atrocities that Jesus suffered at the hand of His opposition, Jesus permitted and allowed suffering, thereby turning those situations into teachable moments.

2. How does Mark 8:31 show that truth?

_____

3. If you have suffered a severe trial or pain, how did you handle it?

_____

_____

4. Did you invite God into your pain to allow His comfort to flow?

_____

_____

We need God's comfort when we experience painful times. In 2 Corinthians, Paul makes clear that only those who have suffered and received God's comfort are properly equipped to comfort others. Inherent in Paul's statement is his overwhelming desire and drive to be like Christ. He joyfully endured the classroom of pain in order to teach the Gospel in meaningful ways.

5. Do you share Paul's desire and drive to be like Christ?

_____

_____

6. What does that look like in your life?

_____

_____

God's provision of comfort is not self-serving but is intended to equip us for service to others and to the Church. God comforts us, Paul states, so that we, in turn, can comfort those in any trouble.

7. As you think on Paul in his circumstances, and perhaps about people in your life who have suffered and yet relied on God for comfort, what overarching attribute do you notice in their lives?

_____

_____

Peace.

As Joel worked through the pain of losing his dad to brain cancer and allowed God to comfort and heal his heart, God's unsurpassed peace replaced his anxiety.

8. Have you walked through a season of suffering and experienced God's amazing peace in the midst of your hurt?

_____

_____

9. How did that affect how you dealt with your situation?

_____

_____

Jesus understood suffering. He experienced the gamut of emotions and suffering while on earth. Yet He had peace. He set His face like a flint on Jerusalem and walked in peace toward the path God laid out for Him. Now that we are in Christ, we can share in His peace.

10. What does 2 Timothy 1:12 reveal to us regarding peace while suffering for Christ?

_____

_____

Walking in God's peace provides us the endurance and patience to run the race marked out for us. Sometimes we easily toss off mentions of divine comfort in the abstract. But for Paul, God's comfort was very real.

11. What comfort did Paul receive in 2 Corinthians 7:4?

_____

_____

12. What about in 2 Corinthians 7:6?

_____

_____

When Timothy arrived, Paul experienced the peace of friendship, accompanied by the good news about the Corinthian Church.

13. How have you received God's peace lately in a tangible way?

_____

_____

Receiving true peace and comfort from God does not mean deliverance from suffering. It provides encouragement in the midst of suffering. Paul was imprisoned when Timothy reached him. Paul received comfort in the middle of discomfort. Paul stressed that offering praise to God for personal comfort received represented only half of the relief equation. He also made it clear that, as God has made us Christ's hands and feet, He uses us to allow God's comfort to flow into those around us. When we approach God's table of forgiveness during communion, we receive refreshment, renewal, and ultimate comfort. That amazing gift allows us in turn to share that refreshment to comfort others.

Our faith journeys remain inescapably intertwined with those of the people around us.

14. Can you recall an instance in your life when your experience of a painful trial has helped you later to walk beside someone else going through a similar situation?

_____

_____

15. How was that comfort received by the other person?

_____

_____

When we suffer, we learn to care. Where nobody suffers, nobody cares. John Henry Jowett, a pastor from England in the late 1800s, once said, "God does not comfort us to make us comfortable, but to make us comforters."

Well said.

We receive comfort in two specific ways:

Directly from God through His Word: Romans 15:4

Indirectly from God through the exhortations of others: 1 Thessalonians 4:18

Christians sometimes neglect meditating upon God's Word and faithful prayer and miss out on receiving God's comfort directly. During Joel's painful struggle with hurt and anger, he blocked out comfort and love from God and everyone else. But eventually, he began poring through Scripture and persisting in prayer. In those holy moments, God mended his pain and healed his heart.

Joel also listened to the wise counsel and encouragement of godly friends. Sometimes we neglect to develop the network of relationships with other Christians through whom God might comfort us indirectly. Withdrawing into isolated bubbles of hurt blocks God's comfort and healing. God knocks on the doors of our hearts to offer comfort. We have the option to open the door. But sometimes we allow anger or bitterness to add another deadbolt to the locked door. In doing so, we miss out on the comfort and compassion God offers so abundantly.

It's important to remember that suffering is suffering. Someone else's suffering doesn't have to match our own experiences for us to empathize, support, and comfort them.

We all have suffered in some way. We cannot use the excuse that since we don't know their exact pain, we're exempt from offering comfort. Offering comfort could be as simple as taking them a hot meal. No in-depth understanding required.

So what will you choose? Will you choose merely to tolerate and endure painful times, or will you choose to permit and allow suffering for the sake of Christ?

God promises we will receive His comfort. Receiving that promise by faith makes all the difference.

Sometimes healing comes in ways and times we're not expecting.

Day 5

WORSHIPING: BASIC COMFORT

When Joel first became a worship leader several years ago, a godly friend took note of Joel's suppressed anger about his dad's death. In brotherly love, he offered Joel advice that changed his perspective: If you struggle to worship God for what He is doing, go back to the basics and worship God for who He is.

His friend's wise advice cracked Joel's brick wall and allowed God access to slay the anger dragon and usher in the healing process.

Anger, among other things, inhibits our wholehearted worship of God. Anger may not be your issue. Maybe you're worried about many things. Perhaps anxiety is your brick wall. But anxiety often wears the mask of anger. Anger masks fear. Fear of failing. Not measuring up. Falling behind. Falling short. Anxiety can make us fierce. The answer?

Adoration of Christ.

We can always find a reason to praise God because God continues to come in grace and mercy, loving and forgiving us, giving everlasting life. Allowing the complications and struggles of this world to turn us away from rejoicing in God's steadfast love for us robs us of intimacy with God. Worship provides comfort to souls battered by difficulties. Although we may be overwhelmed by many troubles, worship vividly reminds us of God's beauty, His love that never fails and His eternal comfort despite our circumstances.

When we worship God using words directly from Scripture, it reminds us of God's amazing promises. Those promises shift the focus from our circumstances onto the One who can change them.

1. How do you see worship and comfort working together in these verses?

Isaiah 25:1

_____

Psalm 95:6–7

_____

2. What is the biggest obstacle we face in worship?

_____

_____

Regardless of the external obstacles that we may struggle with as we worship, the biggest obstacle is what God has to deal with in us—our hearts. Our hearts offer hiding places to harbor unforgiveness, jealousy, rage, malice, and envy, among other toxic emotions. Such emotions barricade our hearts against receiving God's comfort and offering Him genuine worship.

Write the words of Psalm 95:6–7:

_____

_____

3. What do those verses say to you today?

_____

_____

To worship in spirit is to draw near to God with an undivided heart. It means intentional attitudes and actions of focusing on God.

Many of Scripture's prominent figures fell facedown before the Lord in worship when they suffered extraordinarily difficult times.

4. In the following passages, who fell facedown before the Lord, and what were the circumstances?

Numbers 20:6

_____

Joshua 5:14

_____

2 Chronicles 20:18

_____

To worship God in truth means worshiping God not as we *think* Him to be, not as we *hope* Him to be, not as we'd like Him to be, but as He *is*. When we see God as He is, worship flows from a mind renewed by the truth of God.

5. How do you see that truth in the following verses?

Matthew 28:17

_____

Psalm 96:9

_____

The revelation of God's person prompts worship. I can think of no greater comfort than God's amazing presence, can you?

Worshiping in spirit and truth is vital to authentic worship. We find the truth in God's Word. Spending time studying Scripture proves crucial in understanding whom we worship. If our knowledge of God is superficial, our worship will be superficial. If you are in a hurting place and need God's comfort desperately, you don't have time for superficial worship.

6. How does Jesus explain worship to a Samaritan woman in John 4:23?

_____

_____

She came to Jacob's well to retrieve buckets of water. She left with a worshiping heart hydrated by God's unquenchable buckets of comfort and love.

But sometimes when we hurt, we don't feel like worshiping. If I find myself in a hurting place like that, I turn on worship music. At first, I sing along out of habit. I may be doing housework or writing, but before long, I'm no longer just singing. Soon, my brain registers the words I'm singing.

In those holy moments, God allows the meaning of those words to pour over me and ripple against that hurt. Before I know it, I'm singing from my knees as tears splash on the floor. Worshiping as God's comfort gushes in. We may use different things to evade our worship. But God invites us to ditch the inhibitors and approach Him with an undivided heart.

Each week, Joel now encourages our worship team, the musicians, and our congregation to offer our heart inhibitors to God for healing. He invites us to ask God to dismantle the brick walls we've erected around our hearts and allow God's comfort and love to renew us.

God's love is mysterious and relentless and contagious. It may be difficult to grasp when we hurt. But bowing our knees in worship and prayer, receiving His Holy Supper, and opening His Word remind us that He never leaves us. Never forsakes us.

Especially when we hurt.

Lesson 3

SMALL-GROUP DISCUSSION

Joel struggled with anger over his dad's cancer diagnosis, suffering, and death. You may have had a similar experience.

1. Joel's dad was also his hero. Have you ever had a hero? Who? What made him or her your hero?

_____

_____

2. Have you ever struggled with receiving comfort if you believed God caused your discomfort? What was the result?

_____

_____

3. Have you ever put misplaced expectations on someone? What were they? How did it turn out?

_____

_____

4. Have you ever put misplaced expectations on God? What were they? What was the result?

_____

_____

5. In Day 4, we studied the difference between tolerating or enduring suffering and permitting or allowing suffering. Which describes you in this season of your life?

_____

_____

6. When we fully rely on God for comfort during our trials, He gives us His peace. Have you experienced that in your own life?

_____

_____

7. In what ways do you receive comfort as you worship God?

_____

_____

LESSON 4

SHARING SUFFERINGS

Because You're Not Alone

"We share abundantly in Christ's sufferings . . ."
2 Corinthians 1:5

The boy Doug was awake only moments before horrible images began flooding his mind. Snippets of a voice and disturbing sounds assaulted his senses. He desperately wanted to block them out. Erase them forever.

But it had happened.

Again.

As he got out of bed and dressed, his corner beckoned. The only place he felt safe to grieve with the only friend that truly comforted him. The morning light shadowed his steps as he made a path through the dew across the backyard. He called for his trusted companion, who joined him as they headed to his place of refuge. He reached the far outer corner and curled up with his dog. Just trying to forget the images that stained his memory. The smells. The coaxing. He tried desperately to wipe from his mind the events of the night before.

And many others just like it.

Shame and confusion roiled in his brain. But who could he tell? He was only a child. His sexual abuser was someone he once trusted. Who would believe him?

As the abuse continued throughout his childhood, deep-seated anger settled in. *God, why aren't You stopping this?*

Lodged in his heart well into adulthood, his anger affected his marriage, his friendships, and the ministry to which God had called him. Other issues arose connected with his abuse, including depression, behavioral issues, and identity issues. Doug sought Christian counseling for several years to work through the psychological and relational issues that his childhood abuse caused.

One particular session turned out to be pivotal in his healing. After he asked his counselor why God did not stop the abuse, she asked him to picture the room where the abuse took place. "Can you see it?" she asked.

"Yes," Doug replied.

Articulating every word with great care, she said, "Picture Jesus standing in the corner of that room. Can you see Him there? He's crying over the pain you experienced."

The counselor explained that for Jesus to interfere and stop the abusive behavior, He would have had to infringe on the predator's free will. While God doesn't give us free will in spiritual matters, He does give it to us in worldly matters. He gives us free will to choose good in the day-to-day affairs of this life. Because we can make poor choices as we strive to live the Christian life, sometimes God witnesses humans hurting one another.

Over and over.

The counselor further said that if God believed there would have been a better way to accomplish in Doug's life what needed to be accomplished, God would have used it.

But it had to come to that.

In the Garden of Gethsemane, God worked in Jesus before He worked our salvation through Jesus. If God believed there would have been a better way of accomplishing it besides sacrificing His Son, God would have used it.

But it had to come to that.

Now, as a pastor and counselor for more than thirty years, Doug sees suffering almost daily, every heartbreaking situation you can imagine. Destructive words and deeds hurled carelessly, dividing families. Shattering hearts.

Although the childhood abuse he endured was devastating on many levels, he's thankful that God has allowed him to use his pain to help teenagers and adults work through similar issues. His road has not been easy. In fact, he certainly would not have chosen it. We normally don't choose pain.

But now he draws from the wisdom of his personal trauma to speak hope and healing into people's lives with a voice of authority and experience. Not just words that sound good.

As Doug recalls his corner, he realizes that God met him there, although he didn't realize it at the time.

When we hurt, God is still with us.

Capturing our tears in His bottle so that none fall wasted to the ground. May God's Word speak this same hope and healing into your life today.

Day 1

MINISTRY OF PRESENCE

As Doug sat in that backyard corner with his dog, he experienced something we all need. He refers to it as the Ministry of Presence.

The Ministry of Presence occurs when someone simply sits with us in silence as we process our struggles. Doug's wife, Delo, understands his need for this, so when he's processing certain struggles, hurt, or pain, she simply sits in the same room with him. She doesn't say a word, but he knows she's there in case he needs to talk.

1. Do you have a friend or loved one who provides to you a Ministry of Presence?

_____

_____

2. How does that comfort you?

_____

_____

3. How do you feel toward that person?

_____

_____

Whether it's physical abuse, mental abuse, or other suffering, God does not allow or cause pain just to watch us squirm. Like Doug, we may feel alone at our most desperate times, cut off from a world that doesn't know what we're going through. And we're not ready to let them know. Yet.

When we walk through difficult seasons, God faithfully brings forth good out of the bad—if we let Him.

God never forsakes us.

We may not understand or ever see His greater purpose for our suffering, as Paul reaffirms in 2 Corinthians 1:4. But rest assured, His purpose works good in us, and later, *through* us.

Jesus experienced tremendous suffering. He understood loss. He walked through hunger, pain, temptation, hatred, betrayal, and much more. As Jesus hung on a cross with our nails of sin driven through His hands and feet, God turned away from His only Son.

4. What did Jesus cry out in Matthew 27:46?

_____

_____

A holy God cannot be in the presence of sin. During one life-altering moment, Jesus was not just lonely. He was *completely* alone. Forsaken. We may feel like that during painful times, but we are never alone. You and I have a Comforter residing in us—the Holy Spirit—who comforts us from the inside out. If we allow it, His comfort removes fear, calms our minds, and provides much-needed perspective. And Jesus stands as the sin absorber between us and the Father. God sees us white as snow through the red blood of His Son's sacrificial love.

The most powerful, meaningful times that I experience comfort happen when no one else is in the room. When I reach a place of crying out to God and quiet myself long enough to open His Word and listen to Him, His comfort pours into my soul.

5. What does Psalm 46:10 tell us?

_____

_____

That's one of Doug's favorite verses, and mine as well. When you and I take valuable time to process through our struggles with God, He comforts us and moves us to a place where we can offer comfort and compassion to others.

Write out these verses that tell us about compassion.

Colossians 3:12

_____

Ephesians 4:32

_____

1 Peter 3:8

_____

We all have an authentic need for compassion and comfort. We are also called to provide that to others in Jesus' name. Sometimes we struggle with what to say and what not to say when we comfort others, don't we? But God promises that the Holy Spirit has been given to every believer to teach us all things and be our Counselor.

6. What does John 14:26 tell us?

_____

_____

The Holy Spirit serves as our Counselor and Teacher. When opportunities arise for you and me to show compassion, sometimes the best thing to say to someone is nothing at all.

Several years ago, a friend suddenly lost his wife in a terrible accident. I immediately went to their house to be with him, his children, and their close friends. After two hours, when I finally got around to leaving, one person thanked me profusely for the wonderful words of comfort I offered. Yet during the entire two hours, I had only said four complete sentences. What was the comfort they had received?

The Ministry of Presence is powerful and healing.

A listening ear and compassionate heart oftentimes offer the comfort others need without words. Simply being in the same room. Listening. Holding a hand. Sharing a cup of coffee in silence just so that person doesn't feel alone in his or her suffering. The gift of uninterrupted time remains one of our most precious commodities.

It's priceless to bankrupt hearts and spiraling souls.

7. What does John 14:18 promise?

_____

_____

God will come to us as our Comforter—not maybe, not perhaps— He *will*. The King James Version of John 14:18 says, "I will not leave you comfortless: I will come to you."

8. What does that promise mean to you today?

_____

_____

When it comes to comfort, we tend to offer it in the same manner that we prefer to receive it. For instance, Doug finds comfort in the Ministry of Presence. Consequently, when someone comes into his office for counseling and starts to cry, oftentimes Doug will simply allow them time to grieve without wordy interruptions. He offers to them the Ministry of Presence he himself finds comforting.

However, Doug has learned that people may need something different. They may need him to walk them through that grief with advice, words, Scripture, or prayer. Consequently, he has learned to ask, "What do you need right now?"

9. When people are telling you their hurts, have you ever asked that question?

_____

_____

10. If so, did their response surprise you?

_____

_____

Sometimes we assume we already know what kind of comfort a person needs, but we get it completely wrong. When you and I ask hurting people what they need in their moments of grief, they are able to articulate and receive the comfort that speaks to _their_ hearts and temperaments, not ours. We could ask a hurting friend if they want us to pray for them, read Scripture to them, or bring them a meal. Asking, not assuming, provides the best way to truly comfort others.

Our pastors serve as wonderful sources of God's comfort and compassion. Their love for God and the flock God has given them oftentimes offers unparalleled wisdom and personalized care. As we trust them with our trials and fears, we open the door to receive God's reassurance in a tangible way, both one-on-one and in corporate worship.

God comforts each person individually as he or she need it. When I am alone, processing a hurt or grief with God, my comfort often happens through the medium of worship. Music takes my focus off my problem and puts it on the Problem Solver.

Your comfort need may be entirely different. Yet God knows what each of us needs, and He provides it in abundance. God never promised us a painless life or constant sunny skies. He promised to give us the strength we need as we rely on Him for our every need.

What a joy it is to know that the Holy Spirit's presence never leaves us. He offers us comfort and opens our hearts and arms to receive it when we don't have the strength on our own.

Doug knows from firsthand experience the healing power of the

Ministry of Presence. So whether you offer that to a friend or someone provides that for you, remember that our ultimate source of comfort comes from One who is always with us.

In our corners of grief.

Right when we need it most.

Day 2

GRIEF POINTS

Honest grieving isn't pretty. In the movies, we often see someone use one hug and half a tissue to make things all better. But that isn't reality when pain leaves us in a heap on the floor.

As Doug went through counseling to work through his childhood abuse issues, decades of pent-up rage and hurt gushed out. And he discovered firsthand a very powerful truth.

There's healing in the process.

When God moves us from one chapter in our journey of faith to the next, suffering often occurs. In fact, God often uses suffering to advance our faith.

1. What were God's words about Paul's destiny as a servant of the Gospel in Acts 9:16?

_____

_____

As God moves us away from the familiar to prepare us for the next stage of our faith journey, pain gets our attention. It brings us to our knees so that we look up for God's strength and guidance. Sometimes it's hard to function normally when there's a significant amount of pain involved. Several months ago, Doug transitioned to a different ministry area within the church to fully engage and develop it. In the process, he had to leave a particular area of ministry that he deeply and passionately loved. During the transition, he experienced tremendous heartache and feelings of profound loss.

He experienced a Grief Point.

Pivotal, painful events, Grief Points end one chapter in our lives and begin another. They always involve loss. Whether they involve the loss of a person, job, dream, or any other aspect of our lives, Grief Points usher in a new life phase or direction.

Let's look at a few examples in Scripture. Can you identify the Grief Points in these stories?

2. After King David committed adultery with Bathsheba: 2 Samuel 11:13–22

_____

_____

In this instance, David caused his own Grief Point. He had willfully committed a grievous sin, and God took the life of the child conceived in adultery. David grieved greatly. Yet at one point, he decided that sequestered grief was not moving him forward. So he embraced the loss, got up, and started moving toward what God planned for him next.

3. Job, after hearing his children, livestock and possessions had been destroyed: Job 1

_____

_____

Did you notice in this instance that Job had done nothing wrong? In fact, God even called Job a man of integrity, a "blameless and upright man" (v. 8).

4. So why do you believe God allowed Job to experience such loss and heartache?

_____

_____

When you and I suffer painful times, there is always something greater at stake than our happiness or comfort. In King David's instance, God showed that He does not tolerate willful sin, yet forgives those who earnestly seek Him. He told David that his actions crossed the line. A price needed to be paid. And that price was paid by Jesus.

A price needed to be paid to restore fellowship.

And God redeemed King David, who later became known as "a man after God's own heart." Embracing Grief Points and walking toward God in faith is an important stage in fully living out the life God has planned for you.

In Job's case, God sacrificed Job's comfort to demonstrate to the devil and, possibly by implication, us, what a faithful life of service looked like. No matter the pain and suffering Job endured, he never sinned or cursed God because of it.

5. What impact do you believe Job's faith had on those who walked beside him during those trials?

_____

_____

6. Have you ever watched people go through a very painful time in life and yet their faith remained strong and even grew? What impact did their steadfast faith have on your faith journey?

_____

_____

7. What was the result of Job's faithfulness according to Job 42:10–16?

_____

_____

As Job endured such terribly painful times, do you think he believed things would turn out so well? Granted, Job lost his first family and grieved that loss, but God blessed Job because of his unwavering trust in God.

8. When we endure painful suffering, we often do not believe things will turn out well. Yet what does God assure us in Jeremiah 29:11?

_____

Whether the result of our willful sin or otherwise, Grief Points mark significant turning points in our lives that affect us emotionally, spiritually, and sometimes physically.

When our health is affected, we mourn the loss of being able to physically do what we did in the past. For instance, my mom was recently diagnosed with chronic obstructive pulmonary disease (COPD), as a result of being exposed to secondhand smoke. Dad had been a smoker for twenty-five years before he quit. Lung cancer took his life fifteen years later, but as he smoked, the time clock ticked against Mom's health.

When my sisters and I gather to depart on some adventure or just for a day of retail therapy and sister time, we need to regulate walking distances if Mom comes along. She simply cannot walk long stretches because COPD makes it difficult to breathe. Mom grieves the loss of her ability to be active and keep up with her girls.

But her Grief Point also triggers one in me. Her disease alters our caregiver roles. If you have an aging parent, you understand.

9. Have you or a loved one experienced the Grief Point of a limiting health issue?

_____

_____

10. How did you get through it, or are you processing it now?

_____

_____

11. Has someone else's Grief Point ever triggered one in you?

_____

_____

When we experience Grief Points, God's reassurance becomes vital during the transition. As we openly receive His comfort, we look forward to the hope and healing He brings. Relying on God during painful times allows us to look forward to the next chapter in our lives.

But sometimes we get stuck. We don't want to let go of what we have grown comfortable with, so we hold back and choose not to move where God leads. When that happens, we remain trapped in grief by looking at the previous chapter in our lives. There is no particular 1-2-3 recovery process for going through Grief Points. We simply walk in faith, even though sometimes it's anything but simple.

12. When have you had to walk by faith during difficult times?

_____

_____

We obey God by getting up and doing what He has called us to do that day. And we repeat that pattern the next day. Just getting out of bed and going to work, the gym, or church keeps our faith alive, active, and moving forward. Walking in faith is crucial when transitioning through Grief Points. Staying in bed or secluding ourselves from receiving God's comfort in the Divine Service is toxic. The long-term effects plant us firmly in grief if we don't keep moving toward God.

13. What might some of those long-term effects be?

_____

_____

Sometimes we may experience anger as we attempt to discern why God would allow abuse or suffering. But He uses those situations to move us from familiar, comfortable places to stretch our faith. In doing so, He points us to His incredible plan for our lives.

14. We see this exact scenario played out in the life of Abram (later named Abraham). Read Genesis 12:1–8 and record Abram's response to God's calling.

_____

_____

In Abram's case, God provided comfort by promising Abram he would be the father of many nations (Genesis 15:1–6). Abram moved in obedience and God blessed him abundantly. God said go, so Abram went—no questions asked.

But Abram most likely experienced a Grief Point. As he packed up everything and prepared to leave, he was leaving all that was familiar to him, as well as friends and his faith circle.

You and I may face a similar scenario in this day and age when a job transfer moves us across the country. We may leave behind extended family, friends, and a church we feel we cannot function without. Yet sometimes, God has to get us out of our comfort zones to fulfill His calling in our lives. During those discombobulating times, God calls us to walk in faith in the ordinary—packing, moving, and relocating—for Him to bring about extraordinary understanding, healing, and blessing.

15. Can you identify specific Grief Points in your life?

_____

_____

16. How did you handle them?

_____

_____

17. What was the result?

_____

_____

As we experience painful Grief Points, we may feel a sense of being lost or hopelessness. Despite your situation or seemingly insurmountable circumstances, I pray that you cling to God's promises to bring good out of every situation.

Every single one.

As a child, Doug could not see how good could be brought out of the evil of abuse. But today he looks back and sees it clearly. Those painful years helped to shape and mold him into the gifted faith-filled teacher and counselor he is today. He chose to walk in obedience, and, as a result, countless lives have been touched and blessed by the ministry God has given him.

When you and I move in obedience to God's leading, He promises to advance and strengthen our faith in new, amazing ways as we watch Him work in and through us and our circumstances.

If you're experiencing a Grief Point right now, keep walking.

Keep trusting.

Keep moving toward the Comforter.

Day 3

THE INSULATION OF ISOLATION

When you and I experience painful times, we tend to withdraw from people. In Doug's case, he wanted the abuse to stop, but he didn't know whom he could tell. And he knew his abuser might become angry and follow through on scary threats used to keep him quiet.

Sometimes we disengage from family or friends because they are not experiencing our pain. They do not understand, so we isolate ourselves by not leaving the house or refusing invitations to gather. In doing so, we willfully push away the comfort of others.

We become insulated in isolation.

In that dangerous place, Satan does his best work. We are like a lone zebra on the Serengeti, and the prowling lion goes for our throat.

You and I were created to exist in relationship with one another. God knew from the beginning of creation that Adam would need Eve and vice versa.

1. What are God's specific words in Genesis 2:18?

_____

_____

We work better side by side, two by two, and family by church family. Whether or not you are married or have children, God surrounds you with friends and family with whom you can develop meaningful relationships. In those relationships, you learn about comfort and compassion. By definition, comfort is something we *do,* while compassion is something we *feel*. When they work together, they have the power to transform lives.

Throughout his years of pastoral counseling, Doug observed that some people can feel great compassion but cannot offer comfort to others because they're stuck in their own suffering. They're so focused on their own pain and concerns that they don't move forward to comfort others.

For instance, a husband and wife may experience this if they have a wayward child. One spouse becomes overly upset or preoccupied with the pain they feel about their child's direction to the point that he or she neglects to offer much-needed comfort to the other spouse.

Doug sometimes suggests that the husband simply lean over and hug his wife, but often the husband finds himself unable to follow through because he can't move past his own issues.

2. The insulation of isolation damages relationships. How have you seen or experienced that in your life?

_____

_____

Feeling compassion but willfully refusing to extend comfort is self-centered to the core. When we know friends are suffering and we feel compassion, yet do not move forward to comfort them, we have blocked the flow of God's comfort through us.

If you experience times of suffering and withdraw from others, the insulation of isolation represents a double-edged sword. Insulating ourselves gives Satan free reign to mess with our minds. All of a sudden, scary options seem logical. Very few people commit suicide in a crowded room. Our self-imposed insulation also blocks us from receiving God's comfort, a hug from a friend, and even necessary counseling to work through the emotional baggage.

Conversely, sometimes we need to unplug from the chaos of life to listen. In stillness before God, we can sometimes discern the reason for our suffering. Especially if there's sin in our lives that needs to be dealt with.

God may never provide us a clear reason for our trial or pain, but when we spend time with Him, two amazing things can happen:

First, we may hear the uninterrupted voice of God.

Now, I have never heard the audible voice of God, but I have clearly sensed His leading through other ways. Prayer plays an integral part in hearing the still, small voice of God as He speaks to us through His Word.

3. What does Matthew 6:5–14 tell us about prayer?

_____

_____

When we get on our knees before God, it lends perspective to our situation. Although kneeling to pray in church has many benefits, some people do not feel free to be real with God when surrounded by other people. We might think that people will see our confusion and hurt as a lack of faith.

Perhaps we just don't want to admit to someone else that we're hurting.

Instead, we follow Jesus' example and find a quiet place to commune with God alone. In that solitude with Him, we experience the freedom of complete honesty and transparency. When we pour out our hurt, anger, questions, bitterness, or whatever else we're feeling, it releases those toxic feelings in a safe place.

In the arms of Jesus.

4. If you have suppressed hurt, anger, or bitterness, what happened over time?

_____

_____

5. Did you see your feelings surfacing when you least expected it?

_____

_____

When we stuff hurt and anger instead of dealing with it, we turn into grumblers. We do a lot of grumbling sometimes, don't we? For instance, when I transitioned to a law firm closer to home, I joined a group of people who had worked together for many years. Several times, especially in the first few months, I felt excluded from developing relationships with that particular group. Simply put, they were used to operating without me. I grumbled to myself at first before I finally realized that unless I voiced what I felt, they would never know. Over the years, the situation has improved dramatically, simply because of how God led me to deal with it when I poured out my hurt to Him alone.

Instead of isolation, He led me to get involved and contribute to the team in valuable ways. I could have isolated myself and developed the mindset of "me against them," but that would not have resolved anything except to allow resentment and bitterness to settle in my heart.

6. Have you experienced a "grumbling" situation in your life? If so, how did you handle it?

7. What was the outcome?

Many times throughout Scripture, King David grumbled to God. He had enemies pursuing him, and we see his frustration played out in the Psalms.

8. How do these psalms show David handling his difficulties?

Psalm 3

Psalm 36

David knew that when he poured out his pain and suffering before God, God would provide the comfort and strength David needed to get through. David started many psalms venting toward God, but then his words turned to praise for who God is and for His steadfast love for those who love Him.

9. How do you see that in Psalm 77?

_____

_____

10. At what verse do you see the psalmist moving from pain and fear to trust and praise?

_____

_____

11. When you pour out your hurts and struggles to God, do you find that your prayers follow the same pattern as the psalmist's?

_____

_____

Prayer is our first line of action when hurtful events hit our lives. It puts us in a position of listening to God. That takes us to our second significant benefit of being still before God.

God speaks to us through His Word.

When you and I open the Scriptures, we open the means by which we can know and understand God's will for our lives. This also provides the single biggest avenue of increasing our faith.

12. What does Romans 10:17 tell us?

_____

_____

As we read Scripture, we see God's loving, passionate pursuit of us. Over and over we behold a tribe, nation, or people sinning and going against God. But over and over, we see how God provides avenues of redemption.

Pathways of grace. Stepping-stones toward a promised Savior.

The Holy Spirit's gift of faith in God provides comfort to us when life's storms blow through. Believing God is who He says He is and does what He says He will do offers the blessed assurance that our pain is not random.

Our suffering is not secondary.

In faith, we cling to God's promise to love us and draw us to Him.

13. How does God love us according to Jeremiah 31:3?

In His sovereign wisdom, God *chooses* to love us. In counseling, Doug helps people realize the sovereignty of God. Although we may lose our way in seasons of pain, he reminds them that God has a plan. As with Abram in our Day 2 lesson, God always has a greater purpose.

The non-Christians Doug counsels are not open to the unconditional love and purposes of God. They can't figure out why pain is happening if they've been "good," so they focus on a works-based approach: "What can *I* do to make things better?" If we take God out of the equation, we will never find or receive soul-deep, lasting comfort.

When preaching a sermon about the importance of meditating and spending time in God's Word, Doug emphasized that identifying our sin and learning how to stop it does not represent our biggest problem. Rather, it is that we have separated ourselves from God. Sin is our problem. It causes separation and kills us.

He compared it to cigarettes. Cigarettes don't kill us, but they cause the condition called cancer that kills us. God's Word is the ultimate chemotherapy.

We think our biggest problem is sin and learning how to stop it. That's not the issue. Our problem is that we have separated ourselves from God.

Through Jesus we have a bridge to God and away from separation. In the pages of Scripture, we learn how He reconciles us to God, how Jesus seeks us out, picks us up, and carries us like lost sheep back to God. We need Scripture to know about that.

Comfort is not the removal of pain and suffering; comfort is experiencing someone willing to walk through the valley with you. God is always present, and sometimes a few trusted people walk through those valleys alongside us.

But we have to allow that interaction instead of getting stuck in isolation.

Psalm 23 provides a great reminder that God walks with us through the valleys. Psalm 23:2 (KJV) tells us that God "maketh me to lie down in green pastures." He *maketh* us because sometimes that's the only way to get our attention. We tend to go down kicking because our calendars and personal agendas get in the way. We get so busy that we don't take time to be still before Him.

So sometimes, He maketh us.

Our comfort level is not as important to God—our character is His greater concern. For instance, just because a five-year-old is uncomfortable going to kindergarten, the parent won't let him stay home just to keep him comfortable. The parent will make that child go through that experience to learn, grow, and develop character.

God has not called you to live isolated from others or Him.

He calls you into relationship.

With Him.

With others.

Walking through a painful, dark valley can be scary. But during these times, prayer, time in His Word, the renewal and refreshment of the Sacrament, and interaction with trusted friends provide much-needed perspective. These actions allow you to lift your head up and take a breath of fresh air. Relying on God to get you through.

Trusting in His everlasting love.

Day 4

Raising the White Flag of Surrender

During his thirty years in the ministry, Doug has experienced great joy and fulfillment in serving God. He has seen God redeem hardened hearts, turn wayward children back toward their parents, heal marriages, and restore declining health.

Doug delights in providing pathways that develop and nurture other Christians' faith walks. Sitting under his gifted teaching has been a rare privilege. God has used him mightily to bless countless lives. But every now and then, fiery darts pierce him unexpectedly. A thoughtless comment. A sarcastic remark about a passionate sermon.

Anger spewed on him instead of poured out before God.

Serving in ministry requires tenacity and a stiff upper lip. Sometimes ministry takes you to your knees.

In worship.

In tears.

In thankfulness.

1. If you lead or serve in ministry in any capacity, what are your struggles and challenges?

_____

_____

Serving God can break our hearts, but never His Spirit in us. The apostle Paul's ministry expanded across continents, cultural barriers, and religious lines.

And he suffered.

If anyone knew how to open up to receive God's comfort, it was this tenacious apostle. Paul himself provides a quick snapshot of his ministry adventures.

2. What did he face as he served the Lord according to 2 Corinthians 11:23–28?

_____

_____

Serving God today in the United States looks much different than in Paul's day. Yet we still face pain, adversity, hurt hearts, and suffering.

A pastor friend once told Doug that there would be days when Doug would hate his church, his ministry, and he would just want to give up and leave.

3. Have you ever felt that way about your job?

_____

_____

4. How did you get through those times?

_____

_____

But what if your job is your calling? Serving God represents a way of life, not a job. In fact, whether or not you work inside the walls of a church or ministry, your job is precisely where you serve God.

Salt and light.

Shining His light into darkness.

Doug's pastor friend reminded him that when he felt like giving up and walking away, Doug needed to remember his two callings: (1) when Doug felt God calling him into ministry; and (2) the place where Doug received his call to serve his congregation.

When Doug experienced his Grief Point of transition into a different ministry branch (discussed in Day 2), he remembered his friend's wise words.

And he followed them.

Doug took precious time to visit the location where he received his call to become a pastor. That simple yet profound step reminded him of exactly why God called him to serve. Recalling that purpose breathed into him a fresh sense of renewed purpose and affirmation about his calling.

God confirms our calling to serve Him too.

5. How do we see that truth reflected by Paul in Galatians 1:11–24?

_____

_____

Paul knew God had called him to serve in full-time ministry. But suffering was involved.

A lot of it.

Yet, Paul persevered. Most pastors and ministry leaders we think of have persevered.

6. Read through the account of Saul's (Paul's) conversion in Acts 9:1–19. What does Jesus promise in verse 16?

_____

_____

7. In your Christian walk, have you suffered directly from being an instrument for the Lord's service?

_____

_____

As Christians, we share in Christ's sufferings to share and spread the Good News. When we do that, we also choose to suffer. But we are not left alone in our suffering.

8. What does Paul tell us in 2 Corinthians 1:5?

_____

_____

That hope-filled verse affirms that our sufferings will flow, yet Christ's comfort overflows. The sufferings of Christ Paul referred to here are not the usual hardships and tribulations of life, but the sufferings, oppositions, threatenings, and dangers resulting directly from our engagement in the service of the Lord.

So if you've chosen to serve, you've chosen suffering. Jesus made the same choice. But you and I aren't perfect like Him. When our suffering exceeds our capacity to handle it, what does it take to stay the course?

How can we follow God wholeheartedly when sometimes we just feel like raising the white flag and giving up? We walk in obedience.

Obedience.

But you and I tend to push back from obedience. It means someone else sets the rules. Walking in obedience happens when we relinquish control.

Obedience plays an integral part in a believer's journey. We are called to continue walking through the valleys of hurt—especially when it comes to ministry. Hurt-filled people often take their hurt out on pastors. Sometimes life gets messy when serving God in ministry.

Complicated.

Painful.

Our hurt hearts want to curl up in a ball until the world disappears. During those times, focusing our minds to simply walk in obedience proves crucial because sometimes our hearts aren't in it. We may not feel like doing ministry anymore. We may think there's something better out there. But a focused mind overpowers those moments of doubt.

9. What does Paul say about our thoughts in 2 Corinthians 10:5–6?

_____

_____

God meets us on the road of obedience. Walking in faith is the key. Take a moment to carefully read the following passage:

> Answer me quickly, O Lord! My spirit fails! Hide not Your face from me, lest I be like those who go down to the pit. Let me hear in the morning of Your steadfast love, for in You I trust. Make me know the way I should go, for to You I lift up my soul. Deliver me from my enemies, O Lord! I have fled to You for refuge! Teach me to do Your will, for You are my God! Let Your good Spirit lead me on level ground. For Your name's sake, O Lord, preserve my life! In Your righteousness bring my soul out of trouble! Psalm 143:7–11

10. What pivotal words does the psalmist use about walking by faith?

_____

_____

Powerful phrases such as "in You I trust," "make me know," "deliver me," "I have fled to You," "teach me," "lead me," and "preserve my life" reveal how faithfully the psalmist kept his eyes on God for guidance. It's a good example for us.

Even when we're in distress.

If we never experience pain, we will never grasp God's ability to rescue us. We don't look for the rescue; we look for His hand.

11. If God has rescued you from a deep hurt or hard pain, do you remember the rescue or His hand?

_____

_____

But it's not just those in full-time ministry who suffer persecution for the sake of the Gospel. Christ promised His disciples (us) that we would suffer persecution and hardship in the course of serving him. Paul certainly sustained his share.

The English word "sufferings" in 2 Corinthians 1:5 translates the Latin *afflictio*, "to strike on." That is a powerful word picture of Jesus' sufferings as He made His way to the cross of our making.

Christ endured blow after striking blow by whips and fists.

In this day and age, our suffering for the Gospel will not likely take those forms. However, we can be struck in other ways. A harsh tongue, criticism, slander against our intelligence, and more leave marks on us.

12. But when we suffer for the purposes of Christ, He suffers with us because He loves us. What does Psalm 138:8 tell us?

Paul reminds us that the purpose of suffering (or affliction) in Christians' lives is to qualify them for ministry to others. Suffering overflows into us so that we become fellow sufferers with Christ.

13. What do the following verses tell us about this shared suffering?

2 Corinthians 4:10

Colossians 1:24

14. Have you ever stopped to ponder that when we serve others in Jesus' name, we also serve Jesus (Matthew 25:40)?

_____

_____

How does that make you feel?

_____

_____

15. Partnership with Christ in suffering brings partnership in His glory also. What do these verses tell us about that partnership?

Romans 8:17

_____

1 Peter 4:13–14

_____

God's glory only shines through our cracks. As we crack under the trials and heartaches of this life, His goodness and light pour out. Take a moment to write out 2 Corinthians 4:6–10.

_____

_____

We have this treasure shining in jars of clay, so when we break in our suffering, He shines forth from the cracks and holes to dispel darkness.

Yes, we will share in His suffering.

Maybe you're tired of the looks when you admit you follow Jesus.

Maybe you're tired of explaining why you believe what you believe.

Maybe you're tired of Christians lobbing fiery darts at you and other Christians.

I'm thankful to God for using Doug as an amazing, godly example of wholehearted service. Doug prays relentlessly for God to break him in areas of complacency or struggle so that God can use him. He observed:

> Much like the alabaster jar, the more we are broken, the more the fragrance rises up to bless others through what God does through us and our pain.

So instead of raising the white flag of surrender to people, raise your hands in surrender to God's calling on your life.

The suffering hurts.

But it's worth it.

Day 5

CRIMES AGAINST GRACE

As we wrap up our lessons this week, we're taking a different turn. We've spent time over the past several days looking at what we do and how we respond when crimes or hurt are committed against us. Doug's story has given us a powerful glimpse of God's redemption amidst heartbreaking circumstances.

But what if you're the abuser?

You may not be a child predator, rapist, or one who has committed domestic violence, but what if you abuse in another way?

What if you abuse yourself?

Compulsive behavior indicates we have created a stronghold in our spiritual life. The apostle Paul uses "strongholds" to describe spiritual fortresses where Satan and his legions go for protection. These fortresses exist in thought patterns, behavior, and ideas that govern individuals.

1. What does 2 Corinthians 10:4–5 tell us?

_____

_____

Strongholds hold immense power to harm. When we identify compulsive behaviors in our lives, only the mighty weapons of the Word and the Spirit effectively pull down and destroy them.

A stronghold forms when we seek to meet one or more of our basic needs (comfort, security, and love, to name a few) outside of God's design.

We could name many compulsive behaviors, including alcoholism, smoking, overeating, bulimia, cutting, and viewing pornography, just to touch on a few. When we struggle with such issues, we erect a barrier—right in God's face.

As He attempts to pour His comfort into our lives, we deflect it willfully as we attempt to meet those needs without Him.

In other words, we've made our choice.

We don't want any interference.

Especially from God.

Yet He sees everything. He knows everything. We cannot hide.

Believe me when I say that I write these words with the pen pointing back to myself. I've struggled with overeating for years. I understand compulsive behavior.

If you grew up in church, you talked about grace. Sang about grace. Studied grace. Thanked God for it.

2. What do the following verses tell us about grace?

John 1:16–17

Romans 3:23–24

Yet, when we wrestle with strongholds, through the haze of excuses, we realize something terrible: we have abused God's grace.

As compulsive behavior pulls us farther into the dark, our fondness for grace may remain, but our relationship with it changes.

We turn into users instead of partakers.

Perhaps somewhere amidst compulsive behavior, grace becomes little more than an important clause in your contract with God whereby He has to let you into heaven no matter how much your behaviors stemming from your compulsive behavior lead you to sin.

As I came to grips with my compulsive behavior, it rocked my world when I realized how much I had abused God's grace. I had trampled on the blood of Christ. I had been so careless with the gift Jesus died to make mine, I might as well have been finger-painting with His blood.

3. Yet, even in the midst of it, what does Hebrews 4:15–16 tell us?

_____

_____

The New King James Version of verse 16 reads: "Let us therefore come boldly to the throne of grace, that we may obtain mercy and find grace to help in time of need."

Since I didn't grow up in church, the word _boldly_ gives me pause, as does the incongruity of a throne being a place of grace. Thrones are by nature intimidating. From thrones, kings mete out judgments. In some cases, it meant death just to approach one uninvited. We see that most vividly in the Book of Esther (Esther 4:10–11.

4. So when we struggle with compulsive behavior, when we commit crimes against grace, how do we approach God?

_____

_____

Chances are, we approach Him much like a dog who has been caught digging in the garbage—skulking, ears laid back flat, tail tucked in guilt.

5. Have you ever approached God in that way? What were the circumstances?

_____

_____

6. What was the result?

_____

_____

Sometimes our crimes against grace make it hard for us to approach God for grace directly, much less boldly. I mean, when we struggle with compulsive behavior, it seems like that privilege should be permanently revoked.

Yet the stunning truth about God's grace remains: it has nothing to do with us. We didn't generate it. We didn't earn it. We can't buy it. We can't demand it.

We can't lose our right to grace because the right was never ours.

Perhaps compulsive behavior has caused you to believe that grace, if reached for calculatingly, smugly, and selfishly, ceases to be grace at all.

Perhaps your relationship with grace has a rocky history.

But let me ask you, what if God's grace is so great, so loving, so powerful that it's impervious to any human abuse, including yours or mine?

7. Let's allow Scripture to answer that for us.

Romans 5:20–21

2 Corinthians 12:9–10

God invites us to approach His throne boldly. Drinking in grace. Not because of our worth.

But because of His.

If you've struggled with compulsive behavior, you may experience sadness as you think back on abusing God's grace. That when you and I needed it most, we rejected the grace that could have changed everything a long time ago.

To save us from ourselves.

Yet God reminds us in our self-loathing to look up:

Psalm 119:50

Matthew 5:4

Psalm 9:18

Psalm 62:5

Doug's life verse is John 10:10: "The thief comes only to steal and kill and destroy. I came that they may have life and have it abundantly." What Satan comes to destroy us; God comes to give us life.

Abundant grace.

Whether you've abused grace, taken it for granted, or shoved it away, God still provides it.

Ultimate comfort.

In the end, despite our behavior, in spite of ourselves, grace still changes everything.

It always will.

Lesson 4

SMALL-GROUP DISCUSSION

Doug dealt with many issues that arose from his childhood abuse. Now, as a pastor and counselor, he offers invaluable insight on dealing with suffering and grief.

1. In Day 1, we learned about the Ministry of Presence which occurs when someone simply sits with us in silence as we process our struggles. Does the Ministry of Presence comfort you at times? Explain.

_____

_____

2. In Day 2, we learned that Grief Points end one chapter in our lives to begin another, oftentimes involving loss and/or pain. Can you recall specific Grief Points in your life? How did you handle them?

_____

_____

3. Looking back over your life thus far, did you find it difficult to keep walking through Grief Points?

_____

_____

4. In Day 3, we learned about the insulation of isolation. Have you ever pulled back from God and/or those you love when you've gone through a painful season in life? What was the result?

5. In your Christian walk to date, have you suffered directly from being an instrument of the Lord's service?

_____

_____

6. Do you struggle with compulsive behavior? If so, how are you addressing it? Do you have accountability partners?

_____

_____

7. Do you believe we can commit crimes against grace?

_____

_____

LESSON 5

SHARING COMFORT

Even in the Face of Danger

"Through Christ we share abundantly in comfort too."
2 Corinthians 1:5

The hot shower soothed Roxanne's skin, but nothing relieved the ache in her heart. The news her youngest son had shared earlier still reverberated through her soul. She could still picture the resolved look on her husband's face as their son spoke.

This seems so surreal.

Zombielike, she stepped out of the shower, drying off slowly. Mechanically, she looked around her bathroom. Everything looked the same. Yet everything had changed forever.

Was this really happening?

She could feel panic rising in her chest. Crossing the tile floor, she reached for the sink and gripped hard, willing her knees not to buckle. White-knuckled, she leaned against it, as if trying to hold on to sanity. Cling to hope.

I don't think I can handle this.

Looking up, she wiped the condensation from the mirror and met her own gaze.

God, me? The mom of a soldier?

The tears began to flow. She buried her face in the towel to muffle the sobs. Dropping to her knees, she looked up through the haze of hot steam. Through the fog of anguish. As if trying to glimpse the throne room itself, she focused a faith-filled gaze toward heaven.

God, I'll be a soldier's mom if that's what You've asked me to be. But I don't know how. I need Your strength and guidance. Show me how to be a good one. God, please help me.

As she thought back on the previous years, she had known this day would come. Her youngest son, Dan, loved the military. He had graduated at the top of his class from West Point only months before. A bright military future rolled out like a red carpet before him. He was young, intelligent, and a newly commissioned officer. Yet he needed real experience.

Dan had received deployment orders for Iraq.

She thought she could handle the news with grace, offering encouragement to her son for his sacrifice and bravery. But nothing really prepared her for actually hearing the words he had spoken.

"Mom, Dad, they're sending me to the Middle East for a year."

Her world started spinning. She couldn't shelter him. Protect him from harm. A difficult trial for any mom.

As the months unfolded following Dan's sudden deployment, Roxanne and her husband, Scott, prayed relentlessly. Inwardly, her heart hurt for her son because she knew he would see and experience very hard circumstances.

Would the experience harden his tender heart? Turn him away from God? How would he be changed?

She grappled with what her son would see. Actions he would be expected to take. Emotional shrapnel absorbed and perhaps undetected for years.

Roxanne was no stranger to loved ones serving in life-threatening careers. As a mom of three boys, she had been through her share of scares.

Currently serving as a Houston firefighter, her oldest son followed her husband's footsteps in that dangerous career path.

She knew how to be a firefighter's mom and a retired firefighter's wife.

But a son in active combat?

Flames and falling buildings no longer visited her dreams. Vivid, bloody combat images invaded her nights. Images of faceless men targeting the base where he slept.

Dan's danger defined her pain as she imagined every worst-case scenario.

A flag-draped casket shipped home under guard.

A hospital bed holding a burned body or one missing limbs.

Funeral songs accompanied by a twenty-one-gun salute.

Then there were the repeated hellish visions of a black car pulling into her driveway, bearing news that Dan had been killed in action.

Some days, the worry and anxiety threatened to consume her, so Roxanne worked hard at keeping her mind on the ordinary. She focused on her gym workouts. Counting reps brought familiarity. A routine that helped her think clearly. Normalcy that made sense.

Running the gym track served as a welcomed stress reliever. Some days, her heart groaned under the burden of her son's safety. She just kept running.

I'm either going to run until something hurts or until something stops hurting.

Exactly nine months and one week after being deployed, Dan returned home safely, earlier than expected. Although grateful beyond words for her son's homecoming, Roxanne acknowledges with great sadness that some mothers experienced a different result.

Thankful that her son never had to kill anyone, she understands not all soldiers return home untouched by such a burden.

Through the long days and even longer nights, God provided Roxanne daily comfort. People who shared just the right words. Prayed with her. Prayed over her and Scott. And gave encouraging hugs.

Dan is scheduled to deploy again in 2014. And the cycle will start again. With one monumental difference.

She understands now what it takes to be a soldier's mom.

Placing her son's life in God's arms and trusting Him . . . *even in the face of danger.*

Day 1

A SON PRESERVED

As Dan served in Iraq, Roxanne found great comfort when others reached out to her son. The care packages that church, family, and friends shipped overseas meant he would be comforted by reminders of home. Those boxes of love reached out and touched Dan when she couldn't.

Roxanne kept reminding herself that God was in Iraq too. That He was seeing what was happening in the unstable city of Baghdad, as well as in the normal life back home.

This week, we focus on the last part of 2 Corinthians 1:5: "Through Christ we share abundantly in comfort too."

Roxanne suffered a miscarriage early in her marriage, and it played an important role when Dan received his deployment orders. She knew that she would survive mentally and spiritually if her son were killed. She knew what it took to survive the loss of a child.

If you have children, you understand the depths to which you feel your child's pain. Although I don't have children of my own, I see the anguish my sisters go through when their children hurt.

Jesus loved children.

1. What was His response to the disciples when they tried to keep children away from Him in Mark 10:13–14?

_____

_____

2. Children are precious to Jesus. Some women grieve greatly if they find out they cannot have children. If you have experienced that grief, how did you receive comfort best?

_____

_____

Chances are you received comfort from someone who experienced the same grief. Several women in the Old Testament bore the pain of childless years.

3. How did these women handle their grief?

Sarah in Genesis 16:1–5

_____

Elizabeth in Luke 1:5–25

_____

Sarah wanted children so badly that she allowed her servant to serve as a surrogate mother to her husband's heir. Yet Elizabeth did not try to alter God's plan or influence a time clock—and she rejoiced when God's promise became reality.

And then there's the opposite scenario. Some women don't want the children they have. And I don't mean their children are misbehaving. They simply don't want their children.

And the ramifications in those children's lives are epic.

Reactive Attachment Disorder (RAD) is a rare but serious condition that develops when a child's basic needs for comfort, affection, and nurturing are not met, and loving, caring attachments with others are never established. These children are typically neglected, abused, or orphaned.

It is a lifelong, irreversible condition, although the effects can lessen with psychological counseling and caregiver education. A writer friend has an adopted sister who suffers from RAD. When they adopted her fifteen years ago, RAD had not been identified. My friend just knew that her sister didn't like hugs. To this day, her sister doesn't know how to receive hugs, and she has extreme difficulty saying "I love you."

4. Do you know anyone who suffers from RAD?

_____

_____

Science proves what we have instinctively known all along: there's no replacement for comfort. The human touch goes far deeper than physical. It's necessary for development. When withheld, the brain forms differently. Those with RAD have been shown to have brain structures that are visibly different when seen through PET scans.

And there's no replacement for God's comfort. His comfort reaches into the depths of our souls and gives us the strength and courage to handle situations far beyond our own capacity.

Roxanne understands this well. Her experience during Dan's deployment taught her compassion for people who hurt, especially for women who have lost a child—newborn or grown. She realized that she didn't need to experience their same pain to understand their need for simple comfort—a hug, a smile, or a hot meal.

Jesus wanted the little children to come to Him so He could embrace them, pray over them, and delight in them. He knew comfort must be demonstrated.

5. Take a moment to read the following passages and record how healing took place.

Mark 3:9–10

_____

Luke 22:50–51

_____

Luke 6:17–19

_____

A caring, loving touch provides irreplaceable healing and comfort. Roxanne's son was deployed for nine months and one week, exactly the same amount of time she had carried him before he was born. His returning home safely was just as big a moment as when she first welcomed him into the world.

However, labor only hurt for a short while.

His deployment hurt for the whole time.

God preserved Dan while he served in Iraq. Yet His own Son hung on a cross, out of reach of human touch or any comfort, so that you and I could experience comfort eternally.

Thank You, Jesus, for Your abundant comfort.

Day 2

Experience–
The Indispensable Teacher

During Dan's deployment to Iraq, one of the most comforting things Roxanne received was a yellow fleece blanket with the troop support ribbons on it made for her by a friend. Her friend told her, "I wanted to comfort the soldier that never left home." Her friend understood that Roxanne was in the battle just as much as her son was. She would wrap up in that blanket, and it seemed to shrink the miles between her and Dan.

She missed him so much that she often cried while snuggled in its warmth.

As Dan served in Iraq, Roxanne found it difficult to share her pain, anxiety, and worry with others. Simply put, her friends and most family members had never experienced a loved one in active combat. They could only understand her feelings to a certain extent. Most would never ask how she was doing to avoid having to respond to her emotions.

Experience is a powerful teacher. It's also an invaluable tool for offering meaningful comfort. We touched briefly on this in earlier lessons. If you have experienced a deep hurt in your life, it better equips you to offer comfort from a voice of experience.

If you've endured cancer, gone through a divorce, suffered the loss of a child, or watched a parent taken captive by Alzheimers, God wants to use what you learned in the trenches to help others dig out of theirs.

1. What painful situation(s) have you experienced in your life?

_____

_____

2. Has God placed people around you who have gone through similar circumstances?

_____

_____

3. Have you offered to talk with them if they need to talk?

_____

_____

We see clear examples in Scripture of what a friend should *not* do when trying to comfort another friend simply out of lack of experience.

4. Job had three friends. At first they offered Job the Ministry of Presence that we learned from Doug in last week's lesson. According to Job 2:11–13, what did they do when they first arrived after hearing of Job's devastating loss?

_____

_____

5. Job's friends start out well, but then they open their mouths and speak through inexperience. What does Eliphaz tell Job in Job 4:1–9?

_____

_____

6. Don't you wish you had a friend like Eliphaz? Not! But then there are Job's other two friends. What does Job's friend Bildad offer for advice in Job 8:1–7?

_____

_____

7. Again, a gem of a friend, right? But the story and bad advice continue. What does Job's third friend, Zophar, tell Job in Job 11:1–6?

_____

_____

Doesn't that make you want to go out and find such wonderful, comfort-filled friends? Although their intent may have been good (we'll give them the benefit of the doubt), their inexperience led them to offer unstable advice.

Having never had children, I would not presume to tell a mother how to raise her child. I have not done that with my sisters' children, and I won't presume to do it with anyone else. Having never experienced the heart pain that motherhood can bring, I can offer no words of wisdom.

But I can certainly cry with them when they cry and be there when they need me.

8. Have you ever received well-meaning but bad advice from a well-meaning friend? If so, how did you respond?

_____

_____

9. What did you honestly feel about their advice?

_____

_____

10. Did you take their advice? Why or why not?

_____

_____

Jesus understands our suffering. He experienced every kind of pain and temptation when He walked on earth. We can trust His voice of experience.

11. When we hurt and lose our strength to stand for a time, what does He tell us in the following passages?

Psalm 18:31–33

_____

Psalm 28:7–8

_____

Psalm 73:26

_____

Psalm 138:3

_____

Roxanne remembers that while her son served in Iraq, those who helped her the most were people who allowed her to openly express her emotions and talk freely.

As Christians, you and I have our favorite phrases that we like to throw out when people need comfort, whether or not we've ever experienced similar suffering. The comments that helped Roxanne the least were those kinds of thoughtless, safe advice. Can you identify with any of these?

"Just trust God."

"Why don't you try listening to Christian music?"

"Just do Bible study."

Have you ever said any of those to a hurting friend? After experiencing having a soldier in active combat and being on the receiving end of similar unhelpful comments, Roxanne has a new awareness of every word that comes out of her mouth to someone who is hurting.

Tears make other people uncomfortable, so sometimes people trying to offer comfort say anything to turn off the waterworks. Don't fall into that dangerous pattern. Throwing out any of the previous comments assumes that the hurting person is not already doing some or all of them.

Insults don't comfort hurting hearts.

God has allowed certain pain and suffering in your life to be His hands and hugs of comfort to those He places in your path who are going through similar trials.

You may not want to relive your pain, but what you learned in your valley can help them through their similar journey.

And if you don't know what to say to a hurting person, don't say anything.

A hug and the comfort of human touch often provide the best comfort.

Thank You, Jesus, for Your abundant comfort.

Day 3

THE PRAYER CIRCLE OF COMFORT

As she reached for the door handle, Roxanne hesitated.

I don't know some of these women. Am I going to be able to be real about my fears and feelings?

Gathering her courage, she swung open the door and walked in. Perched on various couches and chairs, a handful of women chatted amicably.

The room felt warm and inviting as the women turned toward Roxanne, smiling their greetings to her. It could have been a PTA meeting. A Bible study. An afternoon tea.

But this group of women was very special. They were all moms of sons and daughters serving in active duty in all branches of the military. And they were all there to pray. With one another. For one another. Over their children.

The women started this group in order to offer one another honest camaraderie and abundant comfort through the gut-wrenching worry, anxiety, and loss experienced by military moms. Roxanne heard about the group and knew she had to join.

God, You knew exactly what I needed.

Over the next several months, this prayer circle of military moms became a lifeline of comfort like no other. Comfort flowed uninhibited in that tight-knit group. They prayed and talked openly about their fears, and their children's safety, and they expressed honest, painful feelings without being judged.

1. Have you ever been part of a prayer group? If so, how did it impact your life?

_____

_____

Roxanne believed that if she took her thoughts off of Dan, he would somehow believe she wasn't praying for him—even though he would never know.

But she knew.

So she prayed constantly.

Father, You know the ambushes that await him. Oh, please keep him safe.

2. In your own spiritual walk, how important and relevant is prayer to you?

_____

_____

If we are honest with ourselves, there may be some small part of us that believes this little thing called prayer that we do in this fast-paced, flashy world seems invisible and inconsequential.

But for those who pray and keep their eyes on God Almighty, the miracle movements of His hands are larger than life.

A vibrant and active prayer life teaches us without a doubt that God resides in the details.

3. What does Mark 9:23 say is possible for those who believe?

_____

_____

All things! Everything can be affected by prayer.

Make no mistake: God's plan for His kingdom and eternity will happen exactly as He has planned it. However, there are variables in how that will be accomplished—that's where prayer and faith play an active part.

Notice the active, present-tense *believes* in Mark 9:23 above. We are to continually believe (present tense) that all things are possible through Him and then live that out loud in our faith.

What are we told in Philippians 4:6? But when we face painful seasons in life, giving thanks may be a tall order. When you and I cannot find the words, the Holy Spirit intercedes for us.

4. What does Romans 8:26–27 tell us?

_____

_____

When we hurt, giving thanks may be hard words to form. Yet God instructs us to give thanks.

Even when my son is deployed to active combat?

Even when I can't form words through tears?

Absolutely.

Giving thanks to God as we pray reiterates our humble position as the receiver of His good gifts. Sometimes our situations seem so beyond our control that we can't even see straight to pray about what we truly need.

But if our requests are biblical and line up with God's overall plan, anything is possible.

5. What simple, straightforward instruction appears in 1 Thessalonians 5:17?

_____

When we pray continually, we humble ourselves before the Lord, tell Him our need, and pray for grace and help. Sometimes our situations burden our hearts to such a degree that we can hardly walk through each day. Yet, when our minds stay plastered on God in constant prayer, we receive the strength to function.

Prayer is simply a conversation with God that yields extraordinary results. We can pray anywhere, so our conversation can be ongoing.

For example, my car serves as my prayer closet most days. As I commute to work, travel to speak, or drive to church, that's God time. It's my way of praying and/or worshiping continually. On busy days, my mobile prayer closet (yes, that's really what I call my car sometimes) allows me to pray for many more needs than I would have had time for, sitting still on busy mornings.

6. Do you have a particular place in your home where you go to pray? Do you have a set time for prayer?

Christ dwells in houses of prayer. So how do we build strong houses of prayer?

Establish a time and place. Regardless of where your day takes you, start and/or end your prayers in one place somewhere in your home. Although prayer is not restricted by borders, it still needs an anchor in our homes. A place set aside amidst the hustle and bustle to still the chaos and commune with God.

We need that place to remember.

For our homes to withstand the winds of change and hurricanes of life, we need to make quick stops. Throughout Scripture, we see David and other men of great faith stopping to pray at a fixed hour.

7. What does Daniel 6:10 tell us about Daniel's prayer life?

When the clock struck a certain hour, those seeking after God stopped for Him.

Establishing a time establishes Who the priority is.

God longs for that personal, quiet time with us—His precious creations. In that cherished time of prayer, God directs us, guides us, imparts wisdom, and gives us peace. We see so often in Scripture where Jesus prays to His Father in heaven.

9. How do you see that truth in the following passages?

Mark 1:35

Luke 11:1

_____

John 17:1

_____

Jesus prayed in all circumstances with all kinds of prayers and supplication. But He warned against uttering long-winded prayers simply to impress others. Write the words of Matthew 6:5 here.

_____

_____

Martin Luther, who reportedly prayed on average two hours a day, counseled, "The fewer the words, the better the prayer." Sometimes when we hurt, we couldn't offer a long prayer to save our lives. God hears short prayers, for they, too, take us before our Father in heaven.

Take a moment to write down the following short prayers recorded in Scripture and who said them.

Acts 7:60

_____

Luke 1:38

_____

Matthew 14:30

_____

Psalm 19:14

_____

When I have the privilege to teach Bible classes or speak at various events, I love Psalm 19:14. It reminds me of whom I truly serve.

As we endure suffering, short prayers often reveal our honest feelings and innermost thoughts. When we hurt, we don't like to beat around the bush.

Time is too precious.

Roxanne's military moms circle of prayer provided wisdom and peace at a time she needed it most. They understood time is precious. When news of the war flashed across television screens, Roxanne would freeze, then go home expecting to find a black car in her driveway carrying men with long faces and bad news. Then one of the moms told her about the communications blackout that occurs when a U.S. soldier is killed. Communications about all such incidents are blocked until the families are notified.

After learning that, even though Roxanne held her breath each time she heard that U.S. soldiers had lost their lives, she was able to exhale because she realized that by the time the news hit television, she would have already known her son's fate.

Even though Dan is back safe and sound at his U.S. military post, Roxanne faithfully participates in her prayer circle of military moms.

It's about offering comfort and asking the Comforter to do His miracle work.

Drawing close to God in prayer on a consistent basis is vital to our spiritual health and Christian walk. Only through consistent, honest prayer are we able to live the abundant life of freedom and comfort with the One who created us, who breathed life into us, and who loves us like no other.

Giving God custody of our details makes all the difference in the world. *And around the world.*

Day 4

OVERFLOWING COMFORT

Some days when fearful news about the war in the Middle East seemed constant, Roxanne could not stop the tears. Not only for the loss of lives, but for the families affected. Tears shed for brave soldiers sacrificed in the prime of life.

Her suffering flowed.

God promises that when our suffering flows, His comfort abounds.

Let's start today by writing down 2 Corinthians 1:5.

_____

_____

The Greek verb translated "abounds" means "to exceed a fixed number or measure." If you bake, you can easily picture that concept. When the cookbook instructs us to use a heaping spoonful, we know that means it overflows the sides.

Our suffering may flow, but Christ's comfort overflows.

In other words, when we endure painful trials, God not only delivers us from suffering, but He actually permits the comfort to brim over into our lives.

What does this mean?

In order to identify with Christ, we need to identify with the suffering that served as an essential part of His earthly ministry.

1. What does Mark 8:34 tell us?

_____

_____

Taking up Jesus' cross means painful suffering. He used that specific analogy in teaching the disciples because an instant mental picture popped into their heads.

Golgotha.

The place known as *Golgotha,* "the place of the skull," was located along the main road into Jerusalem. It was the place where crucifixions took place.

Travelers passed right by Golgotha each time they entered and departed the city through its main gate. The location was intentional, of course. The main purpose of crucifixion was not to punish criminals. Criminals could have been punished in any number of ways.

Crucifixion served to deter criminal activity. Wouldn't you think twice about committing a crime if each time you traveled to and from the city, you saw bodies nailed to wooden beams? Heard the desperate moans and cries of the doomed? Smelled decaying flesh and emptied bowels?

Calvary.

Even though Christ's sufferings flow into our lives, His comfort overflows.

Abundant comfort.

This gives us the wonderful assurance that the comfort we receive always outweighs the sufferings we endure in His name.

The same Greek word for "abounds" from 2 Corinthians 1:5 appears many times throughout Scripture. But let's look at one notable instance.

2. Take a moment to read Matthew 14:13–21. What miracle is recorded in those verses?

The last two words of verse 20, "left over," are the same Greek word for "abounds" found in 2 Corinthians 1:5. When the disciples thought they didn't have enough to feed the multitude, Jesus not only provided enough, but He provided an overflow that blessed them with more than they could eat.

3. Have you ever experienced an abundant overflow from God that far exceeded your expectations? What was it?

_____

_____

4. What was the result?

_____

_____

5. How did that incident impact your spiritual journey?

_____

_____

God encourages us in our suffering because the comfort we receive from Him comes through Jesus. This means that all comfort, encouragement, and hope that we receive through the Word, through people, or through circumstances filter straight through Jesus.

We do not have to be stuck in a world of hurt and doubt, because God provides overflowing comfort to His children.

6. How do you see that truth in Isaiah 51:3?

_____

_____

Many hardships and sufferings make the list, but they are covered over by the goodness, comfort, and provision of our God of overflowing goodness.

We do not have to suffer alone or weep in solitude.

God has given us His Word to teach us, the Body of Christ to lift us up, and the Holy Spirit to dwell in us and comfort our souls. And best of all, we have the God of all comfort who longs to show us His mercy and love.

Like Roxanne, we learn through suffering to receive God's comfort through faith with trust, remembering the Lord's blessings, depending on Him, and keeping our eyes on Jesus and Him alone.

As we seek His overflowing comfort when we suffer, Jesus promises, "Come to Me, all who labor and are heavy laden, and I will give you rest" (Matthew 11:28).

Thank You, Jesus, for Your abundant comfort.

Day 5

Normal amidst the Abnormal

As Roxanne embarked on each day, everything appeared to be routine. Quiet time in the Word and prayer. Perhaps some shopping, grocery or otherwise. A gym workout. Volunteer work or Bible class at church. Preparing dinner alongside her husband. Many other ordinary tasks, and lots of projects.

On the outside, everything appeared normal.

On the inside, her heart dwelled in Iraq where her son remained deployed. Her soul lay prostrate before God in prayer. Her mind reeled each time war news hit the television. She spent her strength simply on getting out of bed each morning and walking in faith.

She attempted to appear normal in the midst of abnormal.

Don't you and I put on normal each day to ensure that others perceive that all is well? Do we clothe ourselves in normal, endeavoring to convince ourselves that we are? After all, who set the definition of normal, anyway?

1. Do you believe you are normal? How do you define it?

_____

_____

You and I find a certain level of comfort in normal. We blend in. Nothing seems different. We appear to be just like everyone else. Nothing strange for someone to ridicule. Yet, those difficult seasons in life come around every so often. Times when we undergo a painful trial or experience spiritual warfare played out on a very real stage. War zones make us nervous.

But if we could actually see the spiritual warfare around us each day, it would scare our knickers off.

2. What does Ephesians 6:12 tell us about spiritual warfare?

_____

As God's children, we don't battle "normal." In God's strength, we battle evil and his legions.

During her son's deployment, Roxanne felt numb to being normal. Picturing her son risking his life each day made it difficult to walk the calm streets around her home or church that reflected none of the life-and-death battle on the other side of the world. So she would pray for God's protective armor over her, her son, and all those in danger.

3. What does our spiritual armor consist of according to Ephesians 6:14–18?

_____

_____

God has given us His mighty armor because we face a mighty foe. He visits us in the form of despair. Worry. Anxiety.

Fear.

When Roxanne overheard people being petty about trifles, she forced herself not to point out that the world was so much bigger than whether or not someone's new cell phone had enough memory to hold the latest app.

She wanted to scream at the top of her lungs, "Don't you know that my son placed himself in harm's way to protect the freedom you hold so loosely?"

I wonder how often Mary, the mother of Jesus, thought that very thing. If she observed pettiness around her, I wonder if she wanted to scream at the top of her voice, "Don't you know that my son placed Himself in harm's way to protect the eternal freedom you regard so carelessly?"

The disciples struggled with normal. In fact, they went out of their way to be abnormal in order to draw attention to God's message of hope and salvation they carried.

4. Paul and Silas had been beaten half to death and thrown in prison. What abnormal behavior do you notice in Acts 16:22–25?

_____

_____

5. What was the result of their behavior?

_____

_____

Would you sing in such circumstances? They needed to be different to make an impact. But I wonder if, at that point, Paul and Silas were singing hymns for themselves or for others. When we hurt and suffer, sometimes we sing to remind ourselves of God's faithfulness. The other prisoners just happened to be a captive audience.

Once the truth of Jesus' resurrection stood before the disciples, remaining normal and comfortable was the last thing on their agenda. They needed to be radically abnormal and experience painful discomfort to draw people to a Gospel message carrying eternal ramifications.

6. Have you ever displayed such behavior to serve the same purpose?

_____

_____

7. What did you do?

_____

_____

8. How was it received?

_____

9. What behavior can you identify in the following passages that caught people's attention?

Acts 7:54–60

_____

Mark 15:1–5

_____

If you have said yes to Jesus, you've also said yes to abnormal.

Roxanne's heart hurts over what her son saw during the war. But he won't talk about it. He just wants everything to return to normal.

He doesn't want to answer questions. He believes he was just doing his job—and he continues to do so at his U.S. military base today.

As we close, take a moment to write out the verse that Roxanne focused on each day that helped her live in "normal," even though her son's deployment turned her world abnormal—Psalm 84:7.

_____

_____

_____

When we rely on God's abundant, overflowing comfort, He enables us to go from strength to strength. In His strength.

Because the God of all comfort loves you.

Lesson 5

SMALL-GROUP DISCUSSION

Roxanne suffered through a very painful time while her son was deployed in Iraq. But God surrounded her with the comforters she needed and avenues to deal with her emotions.

1. Have you ever had a loved one serve in the armed forces? What did that cause you to struggle with?

_____

_____

2. Have you ever received well-meaning but bad advice from a well-meaning friend? If so, how did you respond? What did you honestly feel about their advice? Did you follow it?

_____

_____

3. Do you belong to any sort of prayer circle now or have you in the past? If so, how has that comforted you? Are you still in contact with those people today?

_____

_____

4. We learned in Day 4 that our suffering may flow, but Christ's comfort overflows. How have you found that to be true in your life?

_____

_____

5. When we try to appear normal amidst the abnormal, we run into difficulties. How would you define *normal?* On what is is your definition based? God or the world?

_____

_____

LESSON 6

AFFLICTED FOR YOU

Broken to Shine God's Light

"If we are afflicted, it is for your comfort and salvation."
2 Corinthians 1:6

As Annie sat sobbing, her mind replayed the terrible fight with her husband. The words exchanged. The wounds opened. The angry sparring. The ugly faces.

Why did this have to be so difficult?

Curled up on her chaise lounge alone in their bedroom, she slowly regained equilibrium. Jeff had slammed the door and gone outside. They just needed space to breathe right now. Let high-charged emotions subside.

She looked outside the window and turned her gaze toward heaven.

God, I'm so weary.

The fading sunlight peeked through the trees, casting long shadows across the yard. The setting sun painted swirls of vibrant purple and deep pinks across the scattered clouds. The deer would be out soon.

As the tears subsided and calm returned, she thought back over their heated exchange. It always seemed to come back to the same two things: church and money.

She loved one and couldn't care about the other. However, Jeff thought just the opposite.

Annie knew Jeff was a hard worker. As a business owner, he just didn't understand the long hours she devoted to working at a church for half of what she was capable of making elsewhere.

Plus, he didn't particularly care about going to church. He thought they were all the same. Inhabited by hypocrites ready to judge instead of listen. Oh, he had tried attending over the years at different places. But he just couldn't connect. Going to church seemed like a tedious chore better left alone.

Tears welled up in Annie's eyes as she recalled what Jeff finally demanded of her: quit.

He can't be serious, Lord. Please, not that.

She loved working at her church. The people. The teamwork. The mission-minded goals. Never before had she worked at a place where she couldn't wait to get there every morning, work tirelessly and joyfully all day, and regret having to leave at the end of each day.

I just can't bear to leave.

But as she remembered Jeff's arguments and recalled her own schedule, she had to admit it went deeper than just loving her job.

It was driving a wedge into their marriage.

Annie's passion for her job kept her away from home more and more. Some of her ministry duties required evening meetings or attending weekend events.

She was finding it harder and harder to keep up with commitments at home. Simple things such as housework and grocery shopping sometimes went neglected. If there was a family function, it often conflicted with a church obligation of some sort.

As she let her mind wander back over their argument, she could now see something else under Jeff's gruff demeanor and angry words: hurt.

Jeff felt he had been put on the back burner.

Annie tried to defend her position, but deep down inside, she knew he was right. She had not set boundaries. She didn't like saying no to someone at church when they asked her to help.

But God, I feel so close to You and active in Your work when I'm there.

Then she remembered Jeff's profound words: "Working in a church has nothing to do with faith."

And she sensed God's quick response: You can serve Me anywhere. You can shine My light into the world's darkness, but I need you out in it.

She knew right then that to save her marriage, she would have to find a different job.

And her heart broke.

God, what if this makes me hate him?

Day 1

SUBMISSIVE BROKENNESS

As Annie got ready for church, sadness shadowed her face. She would be going alone. Again. Her heart ached that her husband did not share her passion for Jesus. The one thing that represented the central focus of her life.

She struggled at first, having to attend church with their children without Jeff. She was afraid that people would want to know where her husband was. Over the course of their thirty-three year marriage, she had tried everything she could think of to get Jeff, once again, into church including manipulation. She tried suggesting various churches that he might feel a connection to—such as churches other family members attended—in the hope that he would go.

Annie finally gave her hurt and frustration over to God and rested in the knowledge that she wasn't responsible for Jeff's soul—only hers. She had to take ownership and responsibility for her own spiritual walk.

Not Jeff's walk with the Lord.

1. Does your spouse attend church with you? If yes, how does that make you feel? If no, what have you tried to get him to go?

_____

_____

_____

_____

When Jeff finally asked her to quit her job at her church, Annie knew what she needed to do. Submit.

In a study about comfort, submission may seem like an odd topic. But stick with me. The comfort doesn't come directly from the act itself. Comfort comes when we know we have done what God has called us to do.

Write Paul's words from 2 Corinthians 1:6 here.

_____

_____

2. What does "afflicted" mean to you?

_____

_____

In the context of Paul's letter, he and those with him had willingly suffered in order to spread the Gospel message. In relation to our study, if you attend church but your spouse doesn't, your home serves as your mission field. Perhaps your spouse makes fun of your beliefs or makes life difficult when he believes you've put church above his needs.

And so you suffer for the sake of Gospel.

Annie understood that the marriage covenant she made with Jeff was ordained by God. The two had become one flesh. She knew that she could not willfully act in a way that would jeopardize that covenant relationship.

She wouldn't have to answer to Jeff.

She would have to answer to God.

Even though she desperately wanted God to give her another alternative, Annie knew that in order to honor Jeff and submit to his authority, she would have to quit.

3. If you're married, have you ever had to make a similar sacrifice?

_____

4. How did that affect your relationship with your husband?

_____

_____

5. What is your understanding of "submission"?

_____

_____

I know a few pastors who break into cold sweats when they realize God is calling them to preach about submission. They envision herds of angry women making a mad dash for the pulpit with clubs or heading for the parking lot as soon as they get the gist of the sermon's direction.

Women struggle with the topic of submission because in this day and age, it's all about equal rights and fair treatment.

In Paul's day, the Greek word translated as _submit_ was a military term meaning "to arrange [troop divisions] in a military fashion under the command of a leader." In nonmilitary use, it was a voluntary attitude of giving in, cooperating, assuming responsibility, and carrying a burden.

6. Does that definition clarify your understanding of submission? Why or why not?

_____

_____

As women, we need to get our perspective about submission from Jesus Himself. When Jesus faced the final hours before crucifixion, He had a choice. He could have chosen not to face the whip, scorn, and the cross. But He chose to honor His Father by submitting.

Write Jesus' words of submission from Matthew 26:39.

_____

_____

If Jesus had chosen any path other than submission, eternity would not be an option for us. But God knew how He would honor Jesus' ultimate submission.

7. What does Philippians 2:5–11 tell us?

_____

_____

Did you catch the key words of Jesus' mindset and actions? Servant. Obedient. Humble. Emptied.

8. What are God's words to wives in the following passages?

Ephesians 5:22–33

_____

Colossians 3:18

_____

You and I will never be asked to sacrifice as Jesus did. But we are called to that same submission. Whether or not we agree. Whether or not we like it. When we submit to our husbands, we are submitting to God's command in our lives.

If you are married, you're called to submit to your husband. In submitting to your husband, you obey God's command. If you're not married, you submit to God Himself.

Your submission honors God.

9. How do you see that truth in Colossians 3:23–24?

_____

_____

As Annie turned in her resignation at her church, she did so with peace because it lined up with God's Word. Although it was one of the hardest decisions and biggest heartaches of her life, she knew that in honoring and submitting to her husband, she had honored God Himself.

10. Have you ever had to make such a choice?

_____

_____

11. How did it make you feel?

_____

_____

Another way to honor God is with your behavior.

If your spouse does not attend church with you, your behavior has an enormous impact. He gets his impression of Christianity and church from you. If you come home complaining about the music, sermon, the temperature of the sanctuary, or quality of food at the potluck, it simply reaffirms to your spouse what he already suspects: _Christianity is just a façade. They're nice to your face, but they talk about you and behave ugly behind your back._

Your spouse sees and notices everything.

You serve as Jesus' billboard—especially in your home. If you come home talking excitedly about the beautiful music, insightful sermon, and wonderful people, it's only a matter of time before he gets curious enough about it to go. And he can smell a fake at twenty paces. Genuine adoration of God and delight in the place His people gather is the best advertisement on the planet.

16. How do you see that reflected in 1 Peter 3:1–4?

_____

_____

Although never intentional, Annie admits that sometimes she was guilty of letting her church work and service come before her marriage—and sometimes even Jesus. But hearing it from Jeff brought out into the open that truth which had previously remained unspoken.

Submission is the key to unity and harmony in relationships. In marriage, in the Church, or any other relationship, submission represents the basis for unity.

Unity brings comfort.

Annie put it this way:

> Simply living my life of worship and faith has made the difference—not manipulation. Nothing else works. I know because I've tried it all. Honestly loving Jesus, keeping my eyes on God, and wholeheartedly submitting and supporting Jeff are most important. In recent years, I have seen Jeff adore me more as I have honored him more. In those moments, I can see how my submission has built him up so much that now he desires to do the same. There are times when his love for me is so evident, it's overwhelming.

Over the years, she has witnessed the seeds of Jeff's faith growing too. "At mealtimes, he grabs my hand, bows his head, and waits for me to pray." He often listens to Christian music, even sharing with Annie new songs he thinks she would like. When she finally gave up trying to manipulate him, she saw God moving Christian men into Jeff's life who greatly influenced him.

As she honored his request to obtain other full-time employment away from church, she's seen him comforted by the affirmation that she still loves him above a church. It showed him that he was still the most important thing, over anything or anyone on earth.

She finds great comfort in seeing how God waters his faith through her bucket of submission.

Day 2

AFFLICTED
BY SPIRITUAL WARFARE

Several years ago, as they struggled through some very challenging financial difficulties, Annie suggested to Jeff that they do some couple devotions together. So one evening, they settled down together to dig into the Word.

Everything started out just fine, but nothing could have prepared her for what happened next.

"That's the day I realized how much Satan was targeting Jeff."

In the middle of their devotion that day, Annie unleashed an unholy fury at Jeff about their financial situation. The outburst was so extreme and uncharacteristic of Annie that she realized, after she stormed off, that her fury had come directly from hell. Weeping, she experienced disabling terror as she distinctly heard Satan laughing and saying, "You will never get him."

1. Have you ever experienced the terror of Satan's targeted attacks?

_____

After that incident, Annie came to realize that Satan used their marriage as the spiritual battlefield for Jeff's soul.

They went into the devotions innocently. She went in with good intentions. Jeff came out as the casualty of spiritual warfare. It stopped their devotion time for years.

Satan has slithered through the centuries hissing and whispering false promises and lies with one goal: reject God and follow him. The legions at Satan's disposal surround us every day spouting his deception.

The apostle Paul understood affliction. Not just discomfort in general, but specific trials endured for the sake of the Gospel, as we saw earlier in 2 Corinthians 1:6.

The apostle Paul also knew about spiritual warfare. He understood that

Satan has legions at his command to carry out mischief and hurt on God's people. As he penned the letter to the Ephesians, Paul outlined spiritual warfare: who is involved, the pieces of our armor, and in whose strength we are to fight.

Take a moment to write out Ephesians 6:10–11:

_____

_____

From the moment of our Baptism to our last breath, you and I are engaged in spiritual warfare. And it doesn't get easier as years pass. The more effective you become for God's kingdom, the harder Satan works.

Satan actively struggles against God by focusing his energies on shattering the unity of the Church.

Introducing dissention into the family.

Crippling the Body.

Corrupting the Church.

That reality can cause fear in the heartiest of souls, so the apostle Paul introduces the armor of God by focusing on the strength it provides.

In the original Greek, the word in Ephesians 6:10 for "strong" _(endunamoō)_ refers to acquiring strength. In that context, it means to be strong in union with the Lord. We acquire strength through our union with Him. God doesn't simply instruct us to pull ourselves up by our bootstraps and battle in our own strength.

He knows that we would not stand a chance without divine protection.

He has seen our enemy face-to-face throughout the centuries.

Since the battle is spiritual, our armor is also spiritual. We cannot see or hold this armor, but we rely on God's Word and His promise that we have it.

But we have to put it on for it to be effective.

2. What does God tell us about His strength in the following verses?

Romans 4:20–21

_____

Philippians 4:13

_____

2 Chronicles 15:7

_____

Isaiah 35:4

_____

3. According to those same passages, in what specific areas were the believers strengthened by God's power?

_____

_____

Satan knows all of our weaknesses and vulnerable spots and uses fear and doubt to relegate us into ineffectiveness.

But God comforts us by reminding us that endued with His mighty strength, we can stand firm.

We are to rely upon the Lord's strength. Human effort is inadequate, but God's power is invincible. He reassures us that He accomplishes powerful things through us when we depend on the might He supplies.

4. How do the following passages affirm that wonderful truth?

Deuteronomy 33:29

_____

John 14:12–13

_____

5. What comfort do you find in these truths?

_____

_____

Romans 13:14 (KJV) tells us, "Put ye on the Lord Jesus Christ." In putting on Christ and the new person we are in Him, we put on the whole armor of God—the power, might, and strength of our Lord and Savior.

Facing the enemy without His protection is akin to wandering into a minefield without an armored tank.

We are also to stand against the schemes of the devil. _Schemes_ (Greek _methodeia_) refers to deceit, cunning arts, trickery, and wiles. Our English word _method_ comes from _methodeia_. The enemy is methodical in his attacks on us.

6. Our God meets his methodical attacks with specific pieces of armor. Read Ephesians 6:10–18 and list the pieces of God's armor, what they protect, and if listed, their purpose.

_____

_____

Satan assaults our vulnerable spots over and over until he either wears us down or we stand firm in the Lord and prevent him from taking that ground. But God has given us invincible protection—His armor.

7. What comfort does that bring to you today?

_____

_____

We stand in a spiritual battlefield, but God has not left us defenseless! In Ephesians 6:11, Paul uses the plural _schemes_ to define Satan's method.

It reveals that the enemy has unlimited attack plans.

When looking up the definition of *schemes* in *Strong's Concordance,* the reader is directed to "see mischief." If we see anything in the enemy, we see mischief! But his mischief does not come off as cute or coy; rather, it works toward destroying us and diminishing our effectiveness in the battle.

Strong's definition also includes "to lie in wait." That description causes alarm indeed. Satan lies in wait and vigilantly studies us to formulate his attack strategies.

He watches our behavior patterns and points of weakness.

He observes where our eyes are drawn.

He notices how we react in certain situations.

Simply imagining that can send shivers down our spine. Putting on God's armor provides our only defense against Satan's never-ending onslaught.

8. In your life today, how do you see Satan and his legions at work?

_____

_____

Satan is also called "the tempter" (Matthew 4:3) and "the murderer" and "the liar" (John 8:44). Scripture compares him to a lion (1 Peter 5:8) and a serpent (Genesis 3:1; Revelation 12:9), and describes him as as "the god of this age" (2 Corinthians 4:4). This very real enemy possesses vast resources that, thankfully, are limited by God.

9. Satan must obtain permission from God to interfere in our lives. How is that conveyed in the following passages?

Job 1:12

_____

Job 2:6

---

10. Make no mistake; Satan roams and prowls, looking for ways to attack and accuse God's children. How does Scripture describe our enemy in Revelation 12:7–11?

---

11. What comfort does God provide us in Revelation 12:12?

You and I may stand in the middle of spiritual warfare in our homes, marriages, relationships, jobs, churches, families, or friendships. Wearing God's armor makes all the difference.

You and I take great comfort in the assurance that Satan does not have free reign to mess with us. God's protection stands strong and unshakeable as He permits only certain trials that have the potential to strengthen our faith.

If it were up to Satan, Annie and Jeff probably would not be together anymore. Each day they persevere is another day Satan suffers defeat. Annie knows how hard Satan fights to keep Jeff away from God and going to church.

But God faithfully preserves Jeff's generous, compassionate heart and kindness for children and animals in the heat of battle.

And one of these days, who knows?

God just might have big plans for Jeff and his wonderful gifts for His glory.

Day 3

AFFLICTED FINANCIALLY

It isn't surprising that two seventeen-year-old kids suddenly thrown into the grown-up world might have financial difficulties.

So it was with Annie and Jeff. As a young, newly married couple, the world was their apple. And they took a bite every chance they got. They saw money as power. The power struggle over who held the purse strings seemed unending.

As the years passed, they steadily became more independent in their financial decisions, and previous power struggles diminished. They divided the bills, assigning responsibility for each one, and everything rolled along smoothly.

Or so they thought.

Annie and Jeff had very different spending habits. If something caught Annie's eye, she indulged and splurged on the spot. While Jeff did not splurge daily, his indulgences focused on less-frequent, big-ticket items. Hunting trips. Fishing trips. A boat.

They liked material comfort.

1. If you are married, do you and your spouse share the same spending habits?

_____

_____

2. Do you always agree on how money should be spent?

_____

_____

Control of money represents one of the top three marital difficulties. Financial struggles indiscriminately hit people from all walks of life. Married. Single. Young. Old. It doesn't matter. If we do not have solid grounding when it comes to money, it affects every area of our lives.

Most people believe that money brings us ultimate comfort. That if we have money, we won't have problems.

Nothing could be further from the truth.

There were times when Annie used material things to fill an emptiness in her heart. Yet, as Annie grew in her relationship with Christ, she realized He filled in those heart gaps.

Although Annie still loves beautiful things, she has learned that releasing control of her and Jeff's finances to God and relying on His guidance in that critical area ushered in true comfort.

God knew that money would be an issue for His people. He realized that with money came power, and people would want both. So He gave the Israelites one very specific instruction on borrowing and lending that still rings true today.

3. What does Deuteronomy 28:12 tell us?

_____

_____

4. So are you a lender or a borrower?

_____

_____

In previous generations, our parents and grandparents didn't carry debt. They planned, saved, and paid with cash. Having debt was an indication of problems. Today, debt is considered the standard. Oftentimes, the more wealth people have, the more debt they incur. Where is comfort in that?

5. What do the following verses tell us about money?

Matthew 6:21

Luke 12:34

When you pull out your checkbook and see where your treasure goes, does it line up with God's desires or yours?

Annie and Jeff endured extreme financial difficulties when Jeff lost his primary business client. They were building a new house, had a child in college, and spent sleepless nights wondering where the money would come from to meet all of their expenses.

Their relationship suffered because the sudden financial crisis stunned them both. Jeff shut down, while Annie took the reins and steered them out. The collapse of her husband's business was not her fault, yet she paid the price and paid off the debts one by one.

Relationships suffer when money is an issue.

That experience allowed Annie to more fully understand Jesus' sacrifice for us. Jesus paid all our debts and took all the accusations on our behalf, even though our sin was not His fault.

As Annie looks back over that incredibly difficult time, she can see where God provided exactly what they needed financially, precisely when they needed it most. During that time, a friend recommended one particular Scripture passage that sustained her.

Write Proverbs 3:5–6 here.

Annie highlighted that passage and put it in a place in her home where she walked by it every day and read it.

God whispered words of comfort over her through those words.

If you find yourself struggling financially and it's affecting your relationships, there is a better way. Digging out may take awhile, but God promises to provide what we need, when we need it.

6. How is that expressed in 1 Timothy 6:17?

Even though we may not find comfort in denying ourselves the things we want, if hard times hit, we won't find ourselves in a desperate financial situation. Money never provides our ultimate comfort, but placing our hope and trust in God and following His guidance about our finances does.

As a couple, Annie and Jeff looked at their strengths and gifts to decide who would best handles their finances from then on. Annie has gratefully surrendered control to Jeff. He'd learned valuable lessons from the collapse of his business, and he knew he could manage their finances now.

During that process, their power struggle over money disappeared.

Learning that lesson came at a high price, but their marriage and relationship are stronger because of it. Our God is not the God of all comfort only in things spiritual. He comforts us by providing absolutely everything we need.

There is comfort in trusting God with your finances.

Day 4

RESTORATION THROUGH DISABILITY

Having just celebrated thirty-three years of marriage, Annie recalled how God has comforted them, their two children, and four grandchildren. He comforted them through the good times and bad. Triumphs and heartache. Dancing and despair. During those years, Annie sometimes found that love hurts. One of the most difficult challenges in their marriage to date has been having a grandchild with special needs.

Watching their daughter go through the pain, challenges, and heartache of having an autistic child has been very hard. And it's so hard to see their grandchild live with such a disability. But God has used this disability to heal the difficult relationship Annie and her daughter shared. In fact, before the blessing of disability arrived, Annie and her daughter were not even speaking. Then God brought this baby—with all of its problems—to mend their broken relationship. Annie would comfort her daughter by simply listening. Because of the baby's seizures, her daughter was worn out from just dealing with the day-to-day difficulty of caring for an autistic child.

We hurt when our loved ones hurt. It weighs on our minds and tears at our hearts.

God, why can't you just heal them?

Even though we may bristle at the phrase "God's timing is perfect," when we go through difficult times, it is. His timing *is* perfect, in both good and bad times.

1. Take a moment to list some of the ways and situations from Ecclesiastes 3:1–8 when His timing is perfect.

_____

_____

God sees the large picture of our lives and knows the plans He has laid out for us. But we may ask why God allows people to suffer. Let's look at one Old Testament story to answer that question.

After David killed Goliath, Saul's son Jonathan and David became close friends. In fact, take a moment to read 1 Samuel 18:1–4.

David loved Jonathan like a brother, and vice versa. But when King Saul began to fear David and the power David might have over the people, Saul tried to kill David. But Jonathan stepped in, warned David of the danger, talked with Saul, and helped mend the relationship between David and Saul. Through thick and thin, David and Jonathan remained trusted friends.

2. But Jonathan had a disabled son. How did Jonathan's son become disabled according to 2 Samuel 4:4?

After Jonathan's death, David wanted to honor his friend by honoring his family, so he looked for ways to bless Jonathan's memory. He made inquiries and found out about Mephibosheth, Jonathan's disabled son.

3. What does David do according to 2 Samuel 9:1–13?

David honored his friend when he looked past his friend's son's disability to bless him. If you have ever worked with special needs children, you understand how priceless caregivers can be—those caring souls who take care of those children when their parents cannot.

You and I can understand when an accident causes a disability, or perhaps medical malpractice does. We see the circumstances, ascertain blame, and work it out in our minds.

4. But what if that disability exists from birth? Do we blame God? Why or why not?

_____

_____

Disability is referred to in many different ways in Scripture, including "infirmity," "frailty," and "weakness." But I submit that disabilities make us strong. They remind us that we're not invincible. And that we still need a God of healing and comfort.

Mephibosheth's name means "exterminating the idol." Let that definition sink in for a moment. Disability exterminates the idol of physical perfection. Now think of our outward appearance-based culture today.

5. What idol has our culture put on the altar?

_____

_____

I watched a Hollywood awards show recently, and I must confess to being stunned. The red carpet reporters' run down of how people looked, what they wore, and whether or not their outfits suited them left my mouth hanging open.

They discussed who worked out with whom, personal trainers, and the time, effort, and money that went into maintaining their outward appearances. Stunning to say the least.

6. Do you think God is concerned about our physical appearance? Why or why not?

_____

_____

I believe people hyperfocus on appearance because they can manipulate it. They can control it to a certain extent. I can't tell you the number of times I've seen actors on TV after they've undergone facelifts and I hardly recognize them.

But we cannot control God. He works from His own agenda, timetable, and time clock. Many people find that too risky to embrace.

God sees through our disabilities—whether they are physical, emotional, or spiritual—to how He will use them for His glory. Jesus never shied away from those with disabilities and diseases.

7. How do you see that in Matthew 4:23–24?

_____

_____

Jesus didn't have to touch people to heal them. He demonstrated that He can simply speak healing and it happens.

8. How does that occur in Matthew 8:16?

_____

What healed the servant? Jesus' spoken word based on the faith of another person. Not the servant's own prayers and effort. Intercessory prayer is _huge!_

But sometimes God leaves disabilities on purpose.

9. In the following passages, what disabilities do you see in these men of God who were greatly used for God's purposes?

Paul in 2 Corinthians 12:7

_____

Moses in Exodus 4:10–12

_____

10. What reason did Paul give for his disability? What did God tell Moses about his disability?

_____

_____

Both disabilities were intended to bring God praise. Paul defined it as "a messenger of Satan to harass me" (2 Corinthians 12:7). Satan's harassing messengers—demons—harassed God's people in Paul's day, and they still harass us today. We see numerous examples in Scripture.

11. Read the following passages and record who was affected, the disability caused, and how the people were healed.

Luke 13:10–17

_____

Mark 5:1–10

_____

God's love allows us to see a person, not a disability.

Annie realizes that having a grandchild with autism bridged the gap between mother and daughter. Even though the road has been hard, God used that miracle child to mend their relationship. She finds great comfort in knowing that God repaired her family and made it whole again through the affliction—and blessing—of disability.

Day 5

STILLNESS BEFORE
THE SAVIOR

When you are struggling personally, how do you find comfort? For Annie, there's a place in her bedroom near a beautiful window. She sits with her coffee, opens God's Word, turns on soft worship music, and stills herself before God.

She prays.

She reads Scripture.

She listens.

She worships.

I'll admit this week's lesson has been particularly difficult. As we worked through affliction, spiritual warfare, financial troubles, and submission, we're closing out our week just sitting still before our Savior and allowing His Word and presence to comfort us.

Let's start our focus by writing out Psalm 130:5–6:

_____

_____

1. As we turn down the dial of the world's noise and sit still before the Lord to meditate on His Word, how's your heart? Is there anything you are struggling with today? If so, what?

_____

_____

Take this moment to go before God in prayer about your struggle.

_____

_____

In our technological age, it's nearly impossible to be still. Numerous distractions vie for our attention. We seem to have blurred the lines between urgent, important, and what can wait until tomorrow, or even next week.

For some people, stillness and quiet make them uncomfortable. Have you heard anyone say, "I just keep the TV on for the noise so I don't feel alone"? They're not necessarily watching anything. They just want the noise.

Psalm 23 reminds us, "He leads me beside still waters. He restores my soul" (vv. 2–3).

2. When was the last time you slowed down long enough to allow God to do that in your life?

_____

_____

3. What does Psalm 46:10 remind us?

_____

_____

4. What does that verse say to you today?

_____

_____

How does this passage say we benefit by being still before the Lord?

5. Psalm 63:5–8

_____

Psalm 62:1 says, "For God alone my soul waits in silence; from Him comes my salvation." As we look at our calendars, commitments, and obligations, it takes focused discipline to wait silently.

One of the most important facets of our Christian life is the discipline of waiting upon God. That does not mean we live a passive existence. Rather, it means deliberately consecrating ourselves. Listening to the indwelling Holy Spirit.

God refreshes us from the inside out as we still ourselves and discern His will in every given circumstance. As we listen to and follow God's will, He provides His peace that passes all understanding.

When is the last time that you stilled yourself before God? I don't mean when you're sitting in the car at a stoplight. I mean the intentionality of turning everything off at home, finding a secluded spot with His Word, and sitting still before Him.

6. What comfort and peace does that provide for you?

_____

_____

7. When you take time to be still before God, how does that affect your day?

_____

_____

I'd like to share the four specific disciplines I use to intentionally be still before God on a daily basis. Sometimes these happen all together, but more often than not, the first three occur in the morning and the last one in the evening with another time of prayer before I close my eyes.

» I follow a daily Bible reading program.

There are numerous Bible reading plans that we can use. I use a Bible-based software program downloaded to my iPad. Each morning it uploads that day's passages from the Old Testament, New Testament, and Psalms. I click on them, read slowly, and check off each one. Every day without fail, God draws my attention to one particular passage or concept from my morning reading that lasts with me throughout the day.

» I write out a Psalm a day.

I love to write longhand simply because it slows me down. I type like the wind, but in doing so, rich meanings slip right past me. So each morning, I pull out my thick spiral notebook, Bible, and pen and slowly write out one Psalm. Now, of course, Psalm 119 takes a few days, but this Psalm journaling is an ongoing process. When I write the last word of Psalm 150, I start back at Psalm 1. I cannot begin to convey the blessings this discipline has provided. Not only does it slow me down and focus my complete attention on His Word; but I feel His presence so strongly as He whispers the words over me. It is a holy time that I wouldn't trade for anything in the world.

» I pray.

Each day, without fail, I go to the prayer bench in my home library and kneel before God. Believe me when I say that as I head toward that prayer time, the enemy throws distractions at every turn. For instance, this morning, my cat threw up right in front of me as I was walking in to pray. A pretty gross distraction indeed.

» I keep a personal journal.

You may not be a journal person. I understand that completely, I didn't used to be one either. But once I started journaling regularly, I began to see more clearly how God moved through my day as I poured out my hurts, joys, and struggles. He showed me the blessings I didn't notice at the time they happened. I also write down at least five things for which I am thankful that day.

These are just my personal disciplines because I know how busy life can get. It's so easy to simply race from one thing to the next without pausing. But burnout takes much longer to repair than taking the time to be still each day.

Do you have any regular spiritual disciplines you practice?

If not, I pray that you start with one. Pick one and be faithful for one month. It doesn't matter which one you pick because all of them will still you before our Savior. The ways God will speak into your life will amaze you. Then, if you like, add another one. Just keep in mind that it's not how many, it's the quality of the ones you put in place.

As we close today, slowly write out Psalm 37:7.

_____

_____

I pray that His Word works through your stillness before Him to provide you comfort, joy, and His peace that passes all understanding.

Lesson 6

Small-Group Discussion

Like most women I know, Annie struggled with understanding submission when the choice between following God or following her husband seemed to conflict.

1. If you are married, how do you define submission?

_____

_____

2. What does submission look like in your marriage?

_____

_____

3. How have you seen your submission affect the way your husband treats you?

_____

_____

4. When it comes to finances, do you engage in power struggles with your husband? If so, what is the result?

_____

_____

5. Have you ever felt your marriage under attack through spiritual warfare? How did you respond? Did your spouse agree?

_____

_____

6. If you have a disabled person in your family, how has that affected your faith? his or her faith? the family dynamics?

_____

_____

7. Do you spend still time before our Savior? What does that look like in your life?

_____

_____

LESSON 7

PATIENT ENDURANCE

Even When the Storm Rages

"If we are comforted, it is for your comfort, which you experience when you patiently endure the same sufferings that we suffer." 2 Corinthians 1:6

As the elevator stopped on the appointed floor, the short hallway appeared deserted. Expecting the hum of voices and the usual bustle of courthouse life, the sudden quiet sent chills along my raw nerves.

It was 8:46 a.m. The judge's arrival would be promptly announced by the bailiff at 9:00 a.m. sharp. Where was everybody?

I turned the corner and stopped in surprise. The hallway was jammed to the brim with people waiting to enter the courtroom. So many bodies crowded the narrow path that I had difficulty maneuvering toward the door.

Hushed conversations held in stifled whispers sounded like a light wind. Several children stood among the adults, but none was playing. No laughter could be heard. Their eyes stared without blinking at the floor as though transfixed by the tile pattern.

As if moving in slow motion, I took a mental snapshot of that scene. Memorizing each detail. No one wanted to look anyone directly in the eye. Perhaps not wanting anyone to see the depth of pain reflected there that mirrored their own. Or the bewilderment at how they ended up in that hallway in the first place.

With few exceptions, everyone wore black, including me. It looked as if a funeral were about to take place. Ironically, it wasn't just one funeral that occurred there that day, but several.

The Harris County Family Courthouse in downtown Houston experienced death every day. The death of marriages. The cremation of families. The burial place of dreams.

The surreal events of the past four months exploded in high definition as I waited with my attorney to see the judge.

Then everything began moving at speeds only allowed on the Autobahn. My dreams of happily ever after ended less than thirty minutes later as a judge added her signature to the final decree of divorce, looked at me, and said, "Good luck with your new life."

Good luck?

My thirteen-year marriage had blown up, and I never saw the bomb coming. The walls started to close in. I couldn't breathe.

The foundation of my life shook with such violence that the debris threatened to take me down for the count.

The one who swore to stick by me in sickness and in health until death do us part had opted out.

I vaguely remember riding the elevator to the ground floor and stumbling to the nearest bench just as my legs buckled.

I was divorced.

I was alone.

God, help me.

Day 1

THE DEBRIS
OF SHATTERED TRUST

In one earth-shattering morning, my life changed forever. Not the actual day of divorce, but a day four months earlier.

When secrets came out.

Until that morning, I believed my marriage to be strong and solid. Able to withstand any storm, because it had before. After all, he was the one who got me into church. He never gave up or got frustrated with my unending stream of questions about faith, God, and religion.

I was baptized six months after we met, and we married five and a half years later. I had a lot to learn about God, His Word, and His will for my life.

We loved volunteering at church together, especially on the worship team. He had a beautiful voice, so we loved singing together. Everything seemed to be just fine from my vantage point.

But it doesn't take a theological degree to understand trust.

Or what it takes to shatter it.

1. How would you define *trust* in your own words?

According to Dictionary.com, *trust* "refers to reliance on the integrity, strength, ability, surety, etc., of a person or thing."

2. With that definition in mind, whom or what do you trust in your life?

Trust resides at the core of all meaningful relationships. When we trust someone, we feel secure in that relationship. Trust and security comfort us a great deal.

3. According to the following verses, in whom are we to place our trust?

Psalm 4:5

_____

Psalm 9:10

_____

Psalm 20:7

_____

Psalm 37:5

_____

Psalm 52:8 evokes a wonderful mental image of trust: "But I am like a green olive tree in the house of God. I trust in the steadfast love of God forever and ever." Green things live and grow. We flourish when we place our trust in God.

In my mind's eye, I see a greenhouse housing beautiful poinsettias. Outside, a winter storm rages all around it. Inside the security and comfort of that greenhouse, those delicate plants flourish.

You and I can wholeheartedly place our trust in God because He is trustworthy. In this world, we have seen leaders lie, corporations default, churches split, spouses leave, and children abuse.

Is it any wonder why many people have trust issues?

4. What does God promise when we place our trust in Him?

Isaiah 26:3

Proverbs 29:25

Jeremiah 17:7–8

"Blessed is the man who trusts in the Lord." Why "blessed"? Because when you and I trust completely, there is freedom. Security.

A solid foundation on which to stand.

The storms of life can rage, but when we build our spiritual houses on God's solid rock, He enables us in His strength to withstand the howling winds of grief and flying debris of anger.

5. Have you ever had a trust betrayed?

---

6. How did you respond and what was the result?

When trust has been betrayed, the first step is to forgive. That first step may take a long time depending on the depth of that breach of trust and our willingness to turn our hurt over to God.

A friend once said to me that betrayal is much worse than death. No one chooses to die. Betrayal indicates intentionality. Premeditation.

After enduring such a betrayal, I can attest to the truth of that friend's words. A breach of trust at that level does something to you. I began questioning to myself the trustworthiness of everyone around me.

Can you relate?

7. What does Jesus tell us about betrayal in Luke 21:15–17?

_____

_____

Jesus understood betrayal. He experienced it. As He reclined with the disciples during the Last Supper, betrayal sat at the table with Him.

Waiting.

14. Read Matthew 26:14–25. What stands out to you regarding Judas's betrayal of Jesus?

_____

_____

The betrayer wasn't a stranger. Judas was in Jesus' inner circle. He had a relationship with Jesus. He looked Jesus in the eye and still tried to deny it.

I went through a period when I guarded my heart from even those closest to me because I just didn't believe my heart could sustain another devastating blow like that. I felt like the walking wounded.

Some days it felt as if my heart were bleeding out from its wound. I remember thinking it odd that someone could suffer such pain without physical wounds to testify to it.

But guarding our hearts also guards them against receiving comfort from God and those around us. When I let down my guard, God spoke into my heart forgiveness. Healing. A seed of hope that recovery was possible through Him.

But it needed to start with forgiveness.

If you have experienced shattered trust or devastating betrayal, God gives us this hope when we place our trust in Him:

The Lord has anointed me to . . . bind up the brokenhearted, . . . to comfort all who mourn; . . . to give them a beautiful headdress instead of ashes, the oil of gladness instead of mourning, the garment of praise instead of a faint spirit. Isaiah 61:1–3

Day 2

Forgiving to Love

As he walked out of our home the evening a bomb landed in the middle of our marriage, the sound of the door closing behind him ricocheted off the walls.

Is this really happening?

A sound of such desperate pain howled out of my soul that I didn't recognize my own voice. I collapsed where I stood and sobbed. Ugly sobs.

I could hardly breathe.

When betrayal shatters our hearts, how in the world do we forgive? In the middle of hurt, the last thing we want to do is forgive the offender.

We want to stay mad.

Wallow in unforgiveness.

Retaliate in anger.

Seek revenge.

But who does that really hurt? What does unforgiveness solve?

I can tell you from personal experience that unforgiveness hurts us, not the offender, and it solves absolutely nothing.

In fact, unforgiveness harbors toxic feelings that, over time, can turn us into angry and bitter shells.

1. Have you ever bumped into an angry, bitter person? How long did you want to hang around that person?

_____

_____

Forgiveness is so hard that we do not, in our human capacity, have the ability to extend it wholeheartedly. We do not have the strength. But thankfully, God does.

In fact, Jesus understood the power of a bitter, unforgiving heart, so He doesn't just *suggest* that we forgive those who hurt us.

He *commands* it.

2. What do the following passages tell us about forgiveness?

Colossians 3:13

Luke 6:37

John 20:23

Forgiveness is most powerful when it's personal. We can read about forgiveness, listen to others' experiences regarding it, but we do not understand the power of God to heal our hearts until we have to forgive heart-numbing betrayal.

Until we forgive, the hurt becomes the focus of our lives. And the people who caused it become our enemies if unforgiveness stays around long enough. We get stuck in shooting blame at our offenders instead of offering our hurt to God and asking Him to redeem it.

And that brings us no comfort.

We need to start asking God to work forgiveness when the wound is fresh. Before scabs form over our hearts. Jesus displayed an example of this in the most profound way as He hung on the cross.

3. What does Jesus ask God to do in Luke 23:34?

"Father, forgive them for . . ." How would you fill in the rest of that sentence in light of someone who has hurt you?

Jesus was human in every way. As He looked at what transpired against Him, instigated by His friends and enemies, it's reasonable to believe that He experienced the same kind of temptations to resentment, retaliation, and revenge that our hearts would be filled with, given that situation. But Jesus chose not to sin but to call upon the heart of His Father.

That is the first step for us if we are ever to move toward forgiveness. We've got to move past those human tendencies, the brokenness, hurt, and pain, and call upon the heart of our heavenly Father. We release our hurts to Him so that His comfort flows into our hearts.

The Greek word *forgive* used in Luke 23:34 is not the idea of forgiving and forgetting. The word means to intentionally take off. To throw away and not to return to it. In other words, Jesus was saying, "Father, I'm asking You to intentionally take off and remove any sense of judgment or resentment or retaliation against those who have hurt Me. I'm asking You to take it off, lay it down, walk away, and never return to it."

4. When we forgive, what does God promise to us in the following verses?

Matthew 6:14–15

_____

Mark 11:25

_____

Luke 17:3–4

_____

In Matthew, Simon Peter asks, "How many times, Lord, must I forgive someone?" The context is "How many times must I forgive someone for the same sin?" Jesus answers him, "Seventy times seven."

As someone who has experienced a deep betrayal, I can tell you that we will have to forgive many more times than seventy times seven. We have to forgive each and every time we remember, think of, or begin to dwell on that hurt.

And we remember hurt often.

We have to deliberately take it off and hand it back up to God.

You and I are very aware of what has been done to us. But what about what it has *caused* in us? Anger? Fear? Distrust? The hurt inflicted caused those beliefs and behaviors. If we are to truly forgive, we need to just forgive not only what was done, but be willing to forgive what it has caused.

Sometimes we are quick to let people off the hook, totally unaware of the deep scars and permanent wounds that we will live with for the rest of our lives. For true forgiveness to occur, we have to be willing to release what it has caused in us.

The emotional shrapnel that we deal with for the rest of our lives.

If you struggle with unforgiveness, I pray that you get on your knees right now and begin offering those hurts up to God. The sooner you start, the sooner His healing can work true forgiveness in you.

Believe me when I say that I don't offer those words flippantly. I know what it's like to look up from a heap on the floor and ask God through gritted teeth to help me forgive.

Unforgiveness suffocates our hearts and blocks God's comfort from flowing to us.

If you want to live, you have to forgive.

And our faithful God will work that in us if we truly desire it.

Day 3

Valleys of Growth

When I arrived at their house the night my marriage blew up, everything seemed blurry, surreal. My present circumstances. My direction. *My future.*

When Doug (you met him in Chapter 4 of this study) and his wife, Delo, offered to open their home to take me in that devastating night, I knew I had to go. I just couldn't stay in my home alone.

I could still hear the door closing behind him as he left.

I haphazardly threw clothes and necessities into a bag and headed toward their house. I don't remember the drive. I just remember it was raining.

It felt like God was crying with me.

Their welcoming hugs provided such a healing salve to my heart. As they poured love and comfort into my soul, something occurred to me. I wouldn't be going through this alone.

They had actually known my ex-husband longer than I had. They were experiencing their own grief over what had happened.

One of the only things I remember through the haze of pain that evening (besides Delo's wonderful hospitality and Doug's words of wisdom) was Doug's advice to keep a journal as I walked through that dark valley.

As I endured that devastating time of divorce, I faithfully kept a journal from Day 1, and I'm so very thankful. Even though it was hard to remember to take time and write the events and detail my feelings each day, I look back on it now amazed at God's faithfulness.

1. Do you keep a journal?

_____

_____

2. What do you journal? daily activities? prayers? Scripture passages? your journey?

_____

_____

I have learned more about God and grown in my spiritual walk through that particular activity more than any other in my life.

As I prepared to write this study, I removed that precious journal from the shelf and read through it. I cannot tell you how hard that was.

And how much God's healing comfort poured over me as I reread it.

Even though I couldn't see it at the time, God provided exactly what I needed, precisely when I needed it most. Every single day.

3. What do these verses say about God's daily provision for His children?

Matthew 6:31–32

_____

Matthew 7:11

_____

2 Corinthians 9:8

_____

6. Philippians 4:19

_____

First and foremost, I needed God's comfort. I needed His reassuring presence in the midst of devastating brokenness. When I finally settled into the guest bed at Doug and Delo's house that evening, I felt numb. Too much had happened in the span of fourteen hours.

So I pulled out a blank journal and began to write.

My heart bled as ink on the page as I poured out my brokenness to God. I reread my initial entry of that journal and could remember each feeling in detail:

> God, I lay broken and crumbled at Your feet. When he walked out that door, I knew that that sound meant my life would never be the same again. That door closing caused in me an overwhelming sense of loss. Loss of innocence and trust. A betrayal so deep I can hardly breathe from the weight of it. I feel the weight in my soul, but not even fully yet. I know difficult days are coming that are going to cause much more pain. I just want to crawl in bed and sob until I can't anymore. Help me, my Healer. Comfort me, my Comforter. My soul is so sorrow-filled. I need You more than my next breath. God, help me. I'm drowning.

Perhaps you can relate. Whether you experience the loss of trust, innocence, or a different kind of loss, sometimes we endure crushing blows that leave us in a puddle on the floor.

But those puddles of tears hydrate the seeds of our faith.

His life-giving love pours like oil over our heads. He opens wide the faucet of compassion and meets us on the floor. He picks us up, dusts us off, and sets our feet back on the path He has marked out for us.

Psalm 23 offers wonderful words of comfort as we walk through difficult seasons. Write out that entire psalm here:

_____

_____

_____

_____

In the faith that He lovingly provides, we stand in the strength of His might. Nothing in our lives ever remains broken when we entrust the pieces to Him.

When stunning circumstances blindside us, allow those trusted friends God places around you to offer comfort. Open their homes. Take you out for a meal. Take you to the movies.

It's easy to stand alone in pride, but you won't stand long. We need one other when life smacks us down. Don't let pride rob them or you of the blessing of comfort.

Our Savior is the ultimate extreme makeover—heart edition. When we walk in faith through the valleys of growth, keeping our eyes on Him, He creates in each of us a beautiful display of His splendor.

Out of ruins.

Through His love.

Walking by faith.

Giving Him the glory.

Day 4

WALKING BY FAITH

Before I became a Christian twenty years ago, I operated under the false assumption that Christians had a screw loose in their brains.

Just track with me for a minute.

I mean, why follow all of those strict rules if God won't remove all pain and suffering in return? Isn't that just adding to a person's burdens?

Not only did Christians have to continue dealing with life's trials and tribulations, they also had to be sure to walk the straight and narrow, or something really bad would happen to them.

I know that's not a fair statement, but that's what non-Christians believe.

Why pray to Someone you can't see when He's only going to do what He wants to do with your life anyway? I mean, what a serious waste of time, right?

I realize that doesn't paint a pretty picture, but it certainly paints an accurate one.

Then, as a brand-new Christian, I operated under another false assumption; that God would protect me from life's hurts and heartaches. I mean, since He now dwelled inside me, nothing bad could happen, right?

1. If you became a Christian as an adult, did you ask some of those same questions?

_____

_____

2. What answers did God provide that kept you following Him?

_____

_____

One of the first Scripture passages God drew me to as a new Christian was Ephesians 6, where He talks about the armor He provides us. Impenetrable armor that protected from head to toe and everywhere in between. God Almighty had provided me with armor that I could suit up and wear victoriously.

The problem was that I didn't yet realize that I couldn't see the real enemy. The battle resided in the spiritual realm, unseen by the naked eye. My enemy wasn't the person who made me mad at work that day.

I also operated under another false assumption for a long time: God was just waiting to pounce on me and make bad things happen in my life if I stepped a toe out of line. That may sound silly, but believe me, that fear felt as real as getting hit by a car.

I did not yet understand that I stood in the finished work of Christ. I naively believed that I had to work toward being good, never doing any wrong, in order for life to go smoothly. If I didn't mess up, then God wouldn't mess up my life.

Sad, but true.

3. When you hear people say that they are walking by faith, what does that mean to you?

_____

_____

4. What do the following passages tell us?

Hebrews 11:1

_____

2 Corinthians 5:7

_____

Ephesians 2:8–9

_____

Hebrews 11:3

_____

Those verses tell us how vital it is for us to have faith, given to us by Christ. But for new Christians, it can be hard to wrap our minds around some of those verses.

I remember how awkward it was to be a new Christian. Everyone seemed to know so much about the Bible, God, and prayer. I was still trying to understand the basics, so when deep verses about faith surfaced, I felt stupid when I didn't understand.

The point is not for you to feel sympathy or something else for me by reading that. The point is that that's where new Christians start. We talk Christian-ese, and it goes right over their heads.

5. If you know of a new Christian near you, have you befriended him or her?

_____

_____

I learned the vast majority of faith basics from other Christians. Since God's Word still confused me, I listened to other people. How they talked and interacted. What their day looked like as Christians.

Did I match up?

6. What does Mark 10:14 say?

_____

_____

The first time I read that passage, I gained a clear understanding of how Jesus welcomes us. Young. Old. New Christian. Veteran believer.

With open arms.

When new Christians step into church for the first time, I understand what they're feeling. They want to blend into the fabric on the pew and not be noticed—especially if they didn't wear the right thing. They do not—repeat *not*—want to stand and be recognized as a visitor or guest.

They want to hear something that will give them hope. Hope that God loves, not waits to pounce. That God forgives even when we can't forgive ourselves. Something they can apply to their lives today. Not some vague story about a dead person's accomplishments that has no relevance to their struggles.

That may sound harsh, but it's the truth.

So how does all of this relate to comfort?

When people don't understand the love, nature, and character of God our Comforter, they don't feel secure to open their lives and hearts to receive it.

Walking by faith is crucial, but we can't forget those who don't even know where to step.

7. Do you greet new visitors to your church?

_____

_____

If it hadn't been for my ex-husband's commitment to meet me at the front door of church every Sunday, I would not have had the guts to walk in alone. As he walked in faith, he also walked beside me so I wouldn't be left behind in confusion or self-condemnation that I wasn't good enough to enter a church.

8. What does Psalm 119:105 tell us?

_____

_____

When I see people I don't recognize enter our church, I walk toward them with my hand held out. Welcoming them is so very important, because it may have taken every ounce of courage for them to walk through those doors in the first place.

As believers, it is incumbent on us to help those new to the faith find that path of God's light.

So when you go to church this weekend, I pray that you watch for people you don't know. If you don't know many people anyway, it's a great time to start.

Walking by faith produces much fruit for the Kingdom when we walk together.

Day 5

Comfort That Rescues

As the melodic notes floated down the staircase, they told a story.

As a musically wired person, I find great comfort in music. I love to sing and play the flute. Sometimes the comfort comes from a song's Christ-centered lyrics singing into my soul. Other times, it's simply the beautiful melodies and orchestration of an instrumental classic that soothes my soul.

After the judge signed the divorce papers, I have no memory of the forty-five-minute drive home from the courthouse. My stunned mind and traumatized heart had no words.

So I sang. For hours. For days.

I worshiped.

Worship launches us straight into God's throne room, and that's where I longed to be. I knew His comfort would never leave me. Never forsake me.

I worshiped some days until I was hoarse. I praised through tears. I hummed from a heap on the floor.

As I worshiped, facedown in my living room, with carpet hairs up my nose, I had never felt more abandoned in my entire life.

Yet I never felt more loved and cherished by God.

I was never alone.

1. When the darkness of unexpected suffering renders you blind and numb, where do you turn for comfort?

_____

_____

2. The apostle Paul also worshiped when he faced difficult situations. Read Acts 16:22–26. What stands out to you as Paul worshiped?

_____

_____

Paul worshiped even though he and Silas had been beaten half to death. They worshiped while covered in blood and wounds.

When life blindsides us, sometimes we feel just as wounded on the inside. We shuffle along in the dark, groping for hope. Sometimes people aren't available, physically or emotionally, when we need them most. But when we rely on God to provide comfort, we don't have to shuffle far.

As God walked me through the storm of divorce, He imprinted a specific set of verses on my heart. Write the words from Psalm 18:16–19 here.

With the same hands God used as He exerted and displayed His mighty power in raising Christ from the dead, He reaches down from His sanctuary to rescue us when the storms of life threaten to sweep us away in anger, bitterness, and hurt.

These verses remind us that God's grasp cannot be broken. No one can pluck us from His mighty strength. Like baby Moses drawn from the water, God will not abandon us.

Psalm 18:16–19 provides salve to hurting hearts. Did you catch verse 19? He *delights* in us. Why He should delight in us is a question without an answer. A mystery that angels cannot solve.

3. But God repeatedly tells us that He delights in us. How is that expressed in the following passages?

2 Samuel 22:20

Psalm 35:27

---

4. But the delight runs both ways. When we delight in the Lord, what do the following verses tell us?

Psalm 1:2

_____

Psalm 36:8

_____

Psalm 37:23

_____

The Lord establishes the steps of those who delight in Him!

As we walk in obedience during stormy seasons, God promises to rescue us. Just think of Noah. When God commanded Noah to build the ark (Genesis 6:11–21), Noah didn't have the first clue what an ark was. Yet, for decades, surrounded by sand, Noah faithfully built the ark.

But one day, God told Noah to get on the ark because the ride of his life was about to start. Noah gathered his family and the animals two by two and climbed aboard.

Imagine that scene with me. Noah turns for one final look at everything that he had spent his lifetime building and sees the storm clouds rolling in. Hears the thunder in the distance.

Then, as the heavens opened, everything as far as the eye could see disappeared under floodwaters. Don't you think Noah wondered, "Why did this have to happen, God?"

5. When was the last time you asked God that question?

_____

_____

6. What was the result?

_____

_____

You perceive life rolling smoothly, then a drastic event hits with no warning. We lose a loved one, receive a negative health report, collect a pink slip, watch our marriages come to an end, or look on helplessly as our children stray down dangerous paths.

Floodwaters threaten to consume everything.

God promises His children that when we rely on His strength and comfort, we will not be suffocated by destructive spiritual or emotional currents. Regardless of our particular storms, God rescues us and gives us the strength to stand once again. He reaches down with His love and holds on tightly to His dear children.

Though we may notice the wind and waves, God will not let us drown. He brings us through the waters of Baptism and makes us His own. He carefully places us in the ark of His compassion and gives us a brand-new perspective from a grand, spacious place. Why?

Because He delights in us.

That, my friends, provides soul-deep comfort.

Lesson 7

SMALL-GROUP DISCUSSION

As you worked through this lesson, you came to understand a little more about the heartbreak and suffering that comes through divorce. We also talked about new Christians and our charge when it comes to walking beside them.

1. Have you ever experienced betrayal? How did you handle it? What was the result?

_____

_____

2. Have you ever been through a divorce? How did you handle it?

_____

_____

3. If you have ever had to forgive a betrayal, did you find it easy? What steps did you take in working toward extending forgiveness? When you think of that person today, how do you feel?

_____

_____

4. As you have walked through painful valleys of growth in your Christian walk, what kept you walking?

_____

5. Do you keep a journal? If so, how has that affected your spiritual journey? If you don't keep one, would you start one now?

_____

_____

6. How have you experienced God rescuing you when storms hit your spiritual life? What was the result?

_____

_____

LESSON 8

UNSHAKEABLE HOPE

Even in the Face of Addiction

"Our hope for you is unshaken, for we know that as you share in our sufferings, you will also share in our comfort." 2 Corinthians 1:7

Amanda was not prepared for the sight that met her eyes when the door swung open. She almost didn't recognize her dad.

Disheveled, wearing sweatpants, unshaven, and still sporting the hospital bracelet on his right arm, he could barely meet her startled expression.

There was too much guilt. Unbelievable shame.

Another drinking binge had landed him in and out of the hospital.

Again.

Only a few weeks before, Amanda's dad, mom, and brother had traveled down to spend Thanksgiving with Amanda and her husband, Tad. Despite some pleasant times and positive things they were able to share over Thanksgiving, clouds of worry and fear still hung over it all.

Amanda knew that her dad was spiraling down in his disease. Her mom was very depressed, and her brother had no direction after recently losing his job.

Although everything was normal for them, Amanda was no longer happy with that normal.

The week after Thanksgiving, Amanda's parents and brother decided to rent a cottage at the beach about three hours away to further extend their vacation from their icy northern home. Her brother had just lost his job, so the family time and fresh air would do him a world of good.

Amanda returned to work in her position as a kindergarten teacher and life continued as normal.

The week before school let out for Christmas, she called her mom at the beach house and invited her up for the week. Her mom agreed; she needed the escape. Her husband and son wouldn't stop drinking.

That's when everything fell apart.

Amanda's brother, Ray, started calling each day. Some days he was sober. Some not.

"Dad's drinking heavily."

"He won't stop."

"He passed out and I can't wake him up."

"I don't know what to do."

When their dad finally came around, he was severely ill from pancreatitis and diabetic blood sugar spikes. He agreed to go to the hospital, but he couldn't walk to the car. Her brother had been drinking again. He couldn't drive his dad, so they called an ambulance.

After an overnight stay in the hospital, reality finally hit Amanda's dad when he was released.

No one came to pick him up.

Her dad felt completely bereft. He was wearing the sweatpants that he'd worn when the ambulance picked him up. He wasn't wearing shoes. He didn't have his wallet. He couldn't reach his son on the phone.

A cab driver drove him to the beach house to get his wallet, then to the ATM for money, then back to the beach house.

Amanda had heard enough.

She, her husband, and her mom dropped everything and drove three hours to the beach house.

Her dad was livid when they showed up. He said it was none of their business.

As Amanda looked at the shell of the dad she once knew, she felt pity. And it made her uncomfortable.

I don't ever want my children to see me this way.

In that life-altering moment, Amanda felt abandoned. Their roles had changed. Instead of her dad taking care of her, she had to take care of him. She felt overwhelming sadness at the brokenness of her father's life. And he was only fifty-nine.

My life just changed forever.

She couldn't even feel anger toward her dad. He just looked so pitiful. She could feel angry from afar later. Right now, he needed her help.

More than ever.

He tried to be happy. Make jokes. Make light of it. Then his true feelings emerged. As he related his hospital ordeal, he told Amanda that they gave him a little tuna sandwich. At those last three words, he burst into tears.

He realized his addiction had left him abandoned at the hospital. No shoes. No wallet. No one to take care of him. When a nurse realized he hadn't eaten all day, she brought him a little tuna sandwich.

In that moment, he realized he couldn't even meet his own basic needs anymore.

Amanda and Tad paid for all of the prescriptions her dad needed for the next month and convinced her dad to come home with them. That's when the withdrawals started.

Amanda watched in anguish as her dad's blood sugar spiked to over 500 again. He shivered under six blankets. He cried and moaned.

Another hospital stay for four days took her dad to the bottom of the barrel. It was time to change. He kept saying how ashamed he was that his daughter had to see him in such sad condition.

Lord, I need a miracle. Please help me. Show me what to do.

Day 1

Darkness before Light

Amanda's dad got out of the hospital a few days before Christmas. Her family was able to have a relatively normal Christmas, although it was subdued. Everything was going along fine until a few days after Christmas.

Amanda was in the shower when her husband, Tad, rushed in and said, "You better go out and stop your dad. He's in the driveway behind the wheel, trying to leave." Amanda dressed and rushed outside. She begged him not to go back to that beach house where all the liquor was, but her dad insisted that he just wanted to pack up their stuff and return. She made him promise to come back in the amount of time it took to get down there, spend an hour packing, and drive back.

As he pulled out of the driveway, Amanda thought she would never see him again. He was so depressed that she thought he would try to commit suicide again. He'd tried that a few months before. As she watched him drive away, she felt completely helpless. No control at all.

1. Have you ever experienced a similar helpless feeling when dealing with a loved one's problems?

_____

2. How did you feel?

_____

_____

We hurt when those we love hurt. Whether their problems are emotional, physical, or spiritual, it's hard to watch loved ones struggle. We want to take their pain away and restore them. Even with the best intentions, we cannot make someone stop. Whether it's drinking, eating, gambling, or any other vice, at some point that person has to decide for himself or herself that it's time to stop.

As we wrap up our study, we turn our attention to 2 Corinthians 1:7. Take a moment to write that verse here:

_____

_____

3. As you read those words, what stands out to you?

_____

_____

Hope remains unshaken. When we love, hope truly springs eternal. We don't want to give up on them because hope keeps alive the possibility of a better outcome. A better life.

Better choices.

What first comes to mind when you hear the word *hope?* Webster defines hope as "to wish for something with expectation."

4. What does 1 Peter 1:13 tell us?

_____

_____

As we completely fix our hope on His grace, Jesus Christ and His atoning, redeeming sacrifice on the cross stands as our ultimate hope.

5. In your current season of life, where do you fix your hope?

_____

_____

If you're a college student, you may fix your hope on getting good grades and landing a nice job with your degree in hand. If you're newly married, perhaps you fix your hope on starting a family. If you're facing retirement, perhaps you've fixed your hope on a healthy 401(k).

Jeremiah 29:11 promises that God has "plans to give you a future and a hope." As God's people, we have an obligation to live in His hope. Why an obligation? Because we are God's ambassadors here on earth. Others glimpse Jesus through our words and actions.

6. What three things abide according to 1 Corinthians 13:13?

We've heard plenty of sermons on love, and we've read multiple books on faith. But Scripture reminds us with the encouragement to live in hope, as well.

Hope points to the promises of God, ultimately to the promise of that which is eternal (future). We hope for and hope to have what He promises. Faith grasps the promises and reassures us of them now, before we have fully attained them.

Hope means looking to (or longing for) what God has promised to do in the future. Faith believes that God can and will do it because of what He has already done.

Hope expects.

Faith accepts.

So how does that translate into our lives?

» Place your hope in God.

As God's children, our hope does not rest in ideas, people, and the things of this world. Those things will come and go. Rather, we have hope fully, decisively, completely, and to the end in Him who saved us, gives us grace, and will return.

7. What does Hebrews 6:18–20 reveal?

_____

_____

We are to anchor ourselves to the eternal Word of God and His unfailing promise.

His hope is an anchor for our souls.

» We owe our hope to God.

Our gracious and great God sent His Son as the perfect, atoning sacrifice to forgive our sins. Through that redemptive act, God offers us the hope for those who believe by faith in Christ's resurrection that we will not spend eternity separated from Him.

God has been faithful in the past and will be faithful in the future, so we are called to live in the light of that future with Him.

8. God offers us His eternal hope in Him. How is that stated in the following passages?

Colossians 1:5–6

_____

Titus 2:13

_____

Psalm 39:7

_____

Psalm 146:5–6

_____

Hope in God and in His promises should characterize our lives as His children. A living hope in the eternal inheritance God promises to all believers through faith.

» Hope glorifies God.

When we allow our despair over this world's difficulties to rule or overwhelm us, we are saying in effect that we do not trust God. God is glorified when we hope in His future promise, because we are ascribing to God the integrity of that promise.

Our God is a covenant-keeping God who keeps His promises. When we trust God for the future, we are affirming by that trust that God is trustworthy. That faith and trust bring God glory.

9. Abraham is a great illustration of trusting and hoping in God. Read the record of Abraham in Romans 4:16–25. How do you see Abraham's trust and hope displayed?

_____

_____

10. What was the result of Abraham's trust and hope in the Lord according to Romans 4:22?

_____

_____

By all human standards, there was no substance or basis for Abraham's hope that he would be a father, much less a father of many nations. But Abraham didn't trust human standards; he trusted God's plans for his future, and God credited Abraham's faith and trust as righteousness.

Placing our hope in God's promises provides irreplaceable, vital comfort to our souls.

» Nothing but grace.

In 1 Peter 1:13, God's Word tells us exactly on what we are to place our hope: God's grace. The verse doesn't say we are to fix our hope on the end event, on our future reward, or even on Christ. We are to fix our hope on *grace*. It's only by God's grace that we are even able to have faith!

When we first received the salvation of our souls, we didn't deserve it, earn it, or have a right to it; we weren't even worthy of it. It was purely God's gift of grace. Grace is unmerited blessing. It won't be any different in the day of Christ's coming, either. We will no more deserve eternal glory than we deserve the indwelling of the Spirit of glory.

It's all because of God's grace.

Grace is the sweetest, richest, and most wonderful thing there is for a person can ever experience.

11. How is that hope described in the following passages?

Acts 15:11

Ephesians 2:5, 8

---

2 Timothy 1:9

We hope in God's promised plans for our future because by His grace through faith in Jesus Christ, we are able to do so. God does have a plan for our lives—and that promise fosters hope.

12. How have you experienced God's grace today?

---

13. What about last week?

_____

_____

If your joy over your salvation has diminished, if fellowship with anyone here on earth is more desirable to you than fellowship with Christ, it's time to remember the sweetness of God's grace and what awaits us with Him in eternity.

Living in God's grace and in the constant anticipation and hope of His future plans for us with Him is the mark of spiritual maturity. So we fix our hope on God and His grace in our lives. When we do that, God receives the glory He's rightfully due.

During the last four-day hospital stay, God used one particular doctor to bluntly tell Amanda's dad some painful truths: "People in your condition don't leave here [meaning they didn't get released the same night]. You are here because you're an alcoholic. Don't make excuses or blame something else. If you continue to drink the way you've been drinking, you won't have much time left."

As Amanda checked her dad out of the hospital, the doctor offered him this hope: "The damage to your body is reversible if you stop drinking now. Your organs can recover; I don't see cirrhosis. With medicine, your diabetes can be controlled. Alcoholism doesn't have to be the end of your story. You've just got to decide what you want the rest of your life to look like."

Christ's sacrifice on the cross was given to offer us hope eternal.

If you're going through a rough season, it's not the end of your story. _You just have to decide where to place your hope._

Day 2

THE PRICE OF ADDICTION

As far back as Amanda could remember, her dad's alcoholism always existed. Pervasive.

Tainting everything.

As a child, she didn't recognize his behavior as abnormal. Her dad was what is known as a "functional alcoholic." He was just the life of the party—as long as he had a drink in his hand.

She began to realize his alcoholism was not normal when it began to affect her parents' marriage and his health. Hospital visits could no longer be explained away.

Amanda began erecting coping mechanisms to deal with the effects of her father's alcoholism.

She became a fixer.

Her home life was so out of control that she tried to control everything else. Even after she left for college and then moved out of state to begin her adult life, she would help her mom long distance to check on insurance coverage for her dad. She called doctors to warn them of her dad's condition and to ask them to address it with her parents.

1. Do you struggle with control issues in your life?

----

2. If so, what?

----

3. How does that make you feel?

_____

_____

Amanda kept trying to control the effects of her dad's addiction to make them appear normal even though she understood they were anything but normal. She turned into a people pleaser to make people happy. She didn't want to add to her mom's stress by getting in trouble or making bad grades.

Over time, people-pleasing and control issues wear us out. Worse, they can turn us bitter or angry toward those people we may feel the need to please or control.

That brings us no comfort when situations rage out of our control.

If you struggle with control issues, it's so easy to say, "Just give up control to God," but it can be downright grueling to actually that carry out. It takes gargantuan determination.

A good place to start relinquishing control issues is admitting that you are not responsible for fixing or correcting a problem that is beyond your power, authority, or responsibility.

Authority represents a key issue when dealing with control.

As Christians, we confess Jesus as our Lord. In making that confession, we admit that He has authority over everything in our lives. He's both the boss and CEO—the boss who manages people and the CEO who controls all things in every single person's life.

4. What does Matthew 7:28–29 say about Jesus' authority?

_____

_____

Those two verses conclude Jesus' teaching referred to as the Sermon on the Mount, the most brilliant sermon and set of teachings in all of history.

Jesus Himself tells us a very important truth in Matthew 28:18. Write His words here.

All authority has been given to Jesus. "All" means *all*. He alone possesses the power to control people and things. When you and I release those control issue areas to God, He frees us from the sense of obligation to make everything perfect—in our lives and in the lives of those around us.

When we have struggled with control issues over a long period of time, it may take awhile to undo years of self-training. A certain person may instantly ignite the controller in us, so we have to make a conscious decision to give that control over to God each time we see that person or each time those control issue behaviors begin to show up in that relationship again.

It would be extreme to say that you or I plan on becoming fixers or controllers. People don't normally set that as a life goal. Those behaviors normally arise in the context of attempting to bring the normal to abnormal situations.

When faced with insurmountable problems that are out of your reach, allowing yourself to say no or "I can't" goes a long way to handing the authority reins back over to Jesus.

Letting go of the control reins affirms that God is stronger than the individuals or circumstances that are out of your control. He is our ultimate source of power and strength.

5. How do you see Paul affirming that truth in these verses?

1 Corinthians 4:10

2 Corinthians 13:9

Instead of trying to control issues around him, the apostle Paul admitted that his weakness in Christ made him stronger.

6. How does he express that in 2 Corinthians 12:10?

_____

The most freeing aspect of giving control back to God—where it belongs—is that it frees us to love openly. Controlling people or circumstances takes an inordinate amount of time and energy. When we release control and regain that time and energy, we use it to love, help, and serve rather than control.

The Pharisees used religious laws to control the people of Jesus' day. So when Jesus came along and taught people God's truth that opposed their religious rules and practices, the Pharisees challenged Jesus' authority.

7. How do you see Jesus' handling such a situation in Luke 20:1–8?

_____

_____

Jesus didn't waste time trying to explain His authority to people who had no desire to acknowledge or follow it anyway.

Jesus' authority was foretold centuries before Jesus actually walked on earth.

Write Daniel 7:13–14 here.

_____

_____

8. According to the following verses, over what else does Jesus have authority?

Matthew 9:6

_____

Mark 1:27

John 5:26–27

God granted Jesus all authority over people and things, including the circumstances and situations we attempt to control ourselves. Acknowledging and trusting in His authority is the first step in handing over the details of our lives (and the lives of those we love) to Him.

Amanda finds great comfort in taking care of her parents because she has learned to release control to God. Yes, every now and then, those control monsters rear their ugly heads in her mind; but at this point in her spiritual journey, she realizes that the authority to control is not hers.

Her dad's addiction is not her responsibility.

God has her dad in His loving arms.

She trusts God's authority.

And that comforts her to the core.

Day 3

LOVE IN THE FACE OF ADDICTION

As Amanda lay on her living room couch, barely able to function, she kept saying one thing to herself over and over.

Please bring him back.

Her dad had just left to drive back to that beach house he and Amanda's mom had rented, pack up their belongings, and come back to her home.

But all of the alcohol is down there, she kept thinking.

The scene in the driveway broke her heart. She and her husband tried so hard to prevent her dad from leaving without someone accompanying him. That scene replayed in her mind again and again. Amanda feared it would be the last time she saw her dad. He had seemed so desperate.

Taking into account the time it would take her dad to get to the beach house, pack, and return, Amanda made him promise to be back at their house between 5:00 and 5:30 p.m. Eventually, he promised.

And the waiting began.

Amanda lay on the sofa, praying. She had no control. She felt helpless.

But when her dad pulled into their driveway at 5:27 p.m., Amanda could not contain her relief and joy to see her dad alive—and sober. A ray of hope appeared at the end of the addictive tunnel.

Amanda's dad made the choice to attend Alcoholics Anonymous meetings. She decided to go with him. She needed to understand her dad's struggles, the addiction itself, and why it was so strong.

1. Have you ever attended an AA meeting or something similar?

_____

_____

2. What was your impression?

_____

_____

At the AA meetings, within a circle of pain, conversation flows. A sacred gathering of hurting hearts. A holy place. To this gathering, a constant companion comes.

In the middle of the circle, Grief pulls up a chair.

His presence is palpable.

Painful souls share stories, tears, memories. Nothing solved because attempts to do so prove useless.

Grief isn't a problem to be fixed.

It's a presence to be felt.

Those gathered offer one another the only thing they can give: their presence. None of them sits alone with Grief. They draw next to one another in tears. Sometimes in laughter.

Their soul buckets of comfort and compassion pouring into each other.

And God sits with them. Between them. Moving among them. Roaming, embracing, healing.

Jesus understood grief. Write Isaiah 53:3 here.

_____

_____

Jesus and grief are well acquainted.

When we share our grief, we experience the miracle of community. When Amanda first met her husband, she remembers she shared her concern and grief about her dad's addiction.

When Amanda and Tad were married, she was very aware that her dad's alcoholism could be destructive to her marriage. She and Tad were both strong Christians, and they included in their vows, "You are God's special gift to me."

Over the past five years, she has seen that come true in so many ways. Amanda knows that God gave Tad to her as the solid foundation she never had growing up. A rock to anchor to in the storm of her dad's alcoholism.

3. When you think of a strong marriage, what comes to mind?

_____

_____

4. What do the following verses teach about how husbands and wives are to treat each other?

Ephesians 5:22–33

_____

Colossians 3:18–19

_____

These verses stand as the cornerstone of any strong marriage. A marriage that withstands the storms of life. Amanda saw Tad step up and live what he promised to her in his vows. As her dad's battle with alcoholism came to a head, Tad did wonderful things both great and small for Amanda. He was selfless and generous.

Amanda relied on God, but sometimes her dad's alcoholism overwhelmed her. She could not articulate her sadness or speak through her anger, so Tad prayed for her. He prayed over her. He could see those moments in Amanda's eyes. He'd grab her hands and start praying. She thanks God every day for the godly husband He gave to her.

She saw that Tad never became concerned about her parents infringing on his time or space. He wanted to help them as much as Amanda did.

Desperation brings us closer and strengthens bonds when it is faced together.

Amanda realizes that God was with her throughout that horrible day when she waited for her dad to return from the beach house. As she prayed for God to bring her dad back, she realized that God was with her dad too. She said,

> Comfort is knowing that God will carry your loved ones, even when their circumstances, pain, disease, or hurts are completely out of your control. I don't have to fix my dad. I'm comforted in knowing that his Father and mine holds the both of us.

Amanda's dad told her later that he had prayed for God to get him through that trip to the beach house.

God was with them both during their most desperate times.

Pouring comfort.

He does that in your situations as well.

Day 4

VERTICAL FOCUS

As a little girl, Amanda grew up going to church only occasionally. It was just something they did when her parents felt like it. And although they would pray to give thanks at dinnertime and open the Bible on Christmas Eve, Amanda did not see them turn to God for guidance or support.

God just didn't seem to be a priority.

From an early age, she wanted to attend Sunday School. She always knew God was there, but he seemed very, very far away. Too removed from her situation. Amanda strayed horribly during high school and college, even though her grades were 4.0. She would do horrible stuff on Saturday night, then wake up and go to church by herself on Sunday morning.

Yet God was whispering her name.

When she moved to Texas, she met a friend who loved Jesus and her church. You met Amanda's friend, Jennie, at the beginning of this study, in Lesson 1. God, in His divine wisdom, brought Jennie and Amanda together as friends. They were both teachers and secured jobs at the same school.

Amanda had never met anyone like Jennie. Jennie was the first person she had ever met who had a close relationship with Jesus, yet she was not judgmental.

1. Have you ever had a friend like that?

_____

_____

2. How did that person impact your life?

_____

_____

3. What does this friend mean to you today after traveling the friendship road together?

_____

_____

Seeing Jennie live out her faith made Amanda want it too. Before then, she hadn't known that such a thing was even possible. Thanks to Jennie's unconditional love and friendship, Amanda now has a vibrant relationship with Jesus. She loves Bible study.

The more she studied, the more she knew that there were some heart issues she needed to deal with. Anger. Hurt. Control. She longed to be free from those toxic emotions and to receive God's comfort and peace.

So she began asking God to search her heart.

4. What does Psalm 139:23–24 say?

_____

_____

We see King David asking God to search his heart. The man after God's own heart didn't hide his heart from God.

5. What do we see in the following verses about God's heart searches?

Psalm 26:2

_____

Proverbs 17:3

_____

Jeremiah 17:10

_____

Romans 8:27

_____

Did you notice one constant in these passages? God will search our hearts. He does it whether we want to participate or not, whether we agree to it or not. The Creator does not need a warrant or permission to search His created. He has full authority to conduct repeated, thorough, exhaustive, and painstaking investigations.

As Christians, embracing such holy scrutiny is a necessary step toward spiritual growth and maturity. As we read in Psalm 139, we see that David embraced and faced God's examination with eager expectation.

6. What does Psalm 139:1 tell us?

_____

_____

There is an important distinction between Psalm 139:1 and 23. In verse 1, David acknowledges that God has searched him. In verse 23, David invites God to continue to do so.

7. Have you ever invited God to search your heart?

_____

8. If so, what did He reveal to you?

_____

_____

9. What steps did you take to deal with what He uncovered?

_____

_____

Here is a man of courage, determined to explore the recesses of his own heart. As we say in Texas, David wanted to "'fess up."

In biblical language, the heart is the center of the human spirit: from it spring emotions, thoughts, motivations, courage, and actions.

We know the hope of God through our hearts.

13. Read Ephesians 1:18 and 2 Corinthians 4:6. What two specific truths does God say we will know directly because of His enlightenment of our hearts?

_____

_____

Wow! Since God knows us because He searches our hearts, how do we come to know God? Through His Word. As we study and keep our eyes on Christ, God impresses those wonderful truths and promises on our hearts.

11. Spending time studying God's Word is crucial. What does Psalm 119:11 instruct us to do?

_____

_____

Hiding God's Word in our hearts provides one avenue we need to draw close to God, who knows and loves us so thoroughly.

In researching Psalm 139:23, I looked up several different Bible translations of that verse. I was surprised to discover that eight versions used the exact same words. Believe me when I tell you that this is rare—and it clarified without question our assignment to ask God to search our hearts on a regular basis.

Write Psalm 139:23 here:

_____

_____

David was a diligent self-searcher, but he also opened up to be searched by God. He understood the vital difference between searching himself against his own knowledge (darkness) versus being searched by God's refining fire (light). He acknowledged and took refuge in the fact that God's sight is infinitely clearer than his own.

May we receive and believe by faith that wonderful truth as well.

When was the last time that you willingly asked God to search your heart? Pause here and ask God to do just that.

Over time, through studying God's Word and asking God to search her heart, Amanda began to experience dramatic changes in her spiritual walk.

She wanted to work through the past emotional trauma of growing up in an alcoholic home, so Amanda began seeing a Christian psychologist.

That heart-search step transformed her life.

As Amanda began discussing how she had held in past anger and hurt, her counselor suggested that Amanda at least turn to God in simple acknowledgment, even when she was mad at her dad and couldn't really even pray about it. She told Amanda that God would work with whatever she could give Him at the time and help it grow if she would just turn His way.

God, I know You're there. Thank You.

Just that brief thought each day drew her thoughts more and more to God. He started opening her heart and took it from there.

His comfort began pouring in as her healing continues. Amanda's dad still struggles with alcoholism. He will his entire life. But for now, the horizon looks brighter than it has in years.

She has hope.

In that hope, God provides His comfort and peace that pass all understanding.

Day 5

THE CLASSROOM OF ADDICTION

As Amanda grew up in a home with what people referred to as a "functioning alcoholic," she took many notes in that classroom of life. As she watched her dad's behavior and its high price of broken relationships, she realized she had a choice.

In terms of day-to-day living, you and I have the choice to act as we see fit. If we know Scripture, we know how God desires us to live, but you and I are still given the free will to do otherwise. To follow God or not. God gave free will to Amanda, you, me, and Amanda's dad.

1. How would you define *free will*?

_____

_____

Dictionary.com defines *free will* as "free and independent choice; voluntary decision." That pretty much sums it up. You and I demonstrate and exercise our free will several times each day by voluntarily deciding where our feet will take us.

What our eyes will focus on.

What we will choose to listen to.

Our free will affects all things large and small, significant and insignificant. It is all encompassing in scope without regard to rank, status, or background.

2. What does free will look like for you on a daily or weekly basis?

_____

_____

For me, free will means I can choose to take care of my physical body by exercising and eating healthy foods or not. Some days I make those wise choices. Other days I don't even want to talk about.

If you struggle in any area of your life, you understand completely. We find no comfort when we give in to those detrimental behaviors or choices.

Imagine how many parents whose kids are deep in trouble with alcohol or drugs would love to revoke their child's free will. The parents see the hard road ahead, the damaged relationships, the social stigma. But the child only sees one big party.

It makes me wonder how God restrains Himself as He watches us make choices that He knows will result in hurt, pain, and suffering. He looks on as we decide to take another drink.

Inhale another puff.

Eat another piece of chocolate cake.

Visit that Web site.

If you deal with any sort of addiction, free will is one of the most baffling aspects of self-destructive obsession. I mean, if we really get to choose for ourselves, let's ponder this question:

Why can't we just decide to stop?

Of course, it's not that simple. However, it raises an important question that we need to ponder:

Do we lose free will when we become addicted?

Addiction tends to make us think that way, doesn't it? Perhaps a better way to put it would be that our free will gets hijacked and divided by the power of addiction. Once you determine that you truly no longer want to (fill in your vice of choice), and you still do it, you're acting against your own will.

The one of you has split into two.

3. How did the apostle Paul phrase his frustration with free will in Romans 7:14–19?

_____

_____

We don't know for sure whether the apostle Paul struggled with an addiction of some kind, but it sure sounds similar, doesn't it?

4. Write down his answer from Romans 7:20:

_____

_____

5. It's almost as if Paul is saying, "Sin made me do it. It wasn't really me." How would you paraphrase Paul's words?

_____

_____

Addiction is a direct result of free will. Psychologists study such behavior in careful detail. Perhaps understanding that addiction divides us against ourselves helps to explain why it is so incredibly powerful.

Simply put, we don't wake up one morning and decide to be an alcoholic or meth addict and then outline the steps to reach that goal. Becoming any kind of addict is the result of free-will choices that grew more harmful as time went by.

But admitting addiction is only half of it.

You have to do something about it.

Have you noticed? Some addictions seem to be more addictions than others? For instance, being addicted to food doesn't carry a fraction of the unacceptable stigma of drug addiction. Being addicted to work doesn't measure up to the stigma of being a raging alcoholic.

Free will can sometimes take our paths very far from where God originally intended. By allowing us to suffer the consequences of our decisions, God causes enough pain to get our attention. But He still promises to pull us out of the pit and put our feet back on His rock.

6. How is that promise described in the following passages?

2 Samuel 22:17–20

_____

Psalm 18:16–19

_____

God promises that He reaches down to rescue us from the deep waters that threaten to consume us. Even the floodwaters of addiction.

How do you win the addiction battle when every ounce of your self-will and self-reliance is shared by the addict in you? After all, don't you share the same free will?

7. What are your thoughts?

_____

_____

8. Obviously, if our free will itself is divided, willpower or simply "trying harder" is not the answer. Write Paul's words of frustration about this from Romans 7:24 here.

_____

_____

Paul knew he wanted to make better decisions, but he seemed held captive by his own free will and sinful nature. You and I can certainly identify with that.

Hope and comfort arrive when we come to a place of fully surrendering our entire will over to God. Every day. Sometimes, every hour.

9. What does Matthew 6:24–34 tell us about surrendering our will to God?

_____

_____

For some, like Amanda's dad, that means hitting the bottom of the barrel. But some of us have many levels in the barrel. Many different bottoms to slide toward.

When we pray "Thy will be done," we pray that God would break our sinful wills and conform them to His holy will for us. As He breaks our sinful wills by conforming them to His will do we do we finally find comfort and freedom.

I don't know about you, but I'm grateful for free will. Despite how much it sets us up for heartache, it also reintroduces us to God's love and compassion when we make bad decisions.

It invites us to hope.

It means we can still say yes to rescue.

Yes to grace.

Yes as a prodigal coming home to our heavenly Father.

Again and again.

Amanda exercised her free will to stop the cycle of heartbreaking, life-altering alcoholism. And through her experience, God has prepared her to help others dealing with similar situations—and perhaps, help them avoid her dad's painful, addictive path.

She acknowledges that everyone has their struggles, and by the grace of God, alcoholism just doesn't happen to be hers.

Receiving God's comfort through dealing with her dad's alcoholism allows her to offer compassion from personal experience and deep empathy. She willfully chooses to pour God's encouragement, comfort, and hope into others.

May we exercise our free will to do likewise.

"Our hope for you is unshaken, for we know that as you share in our sufferings, you will also share in our comfort." 2 Corinthians 1:7

Lesson 8

SMALL-GROUP DISCUSSION

Amanda has struggled with her dad's addiction to alcohol for all of her life. It has affected her emotionally and spiritually, and it has impacted her family in many ways.

1. Do you have a loved one who struggles with an addiction or compulsive behavior? How does he or she deal with it? How do you deal with it? Do you ever try discussing it with him or her? How does he or she respond?

_____

_____

2. If that person is a close loved one, how do you deal with your feelings of helplessness?

_____

_____

3. Do you struggle with control issues in your life? What brought on that behavior?

_____

_____

4. Do you have authority issues when it comes to God?

_____

_____

5. When you think of a strong marriage in the face of addiction, what comes to mind? What is the main thing spouses could do for each other when struggling with a family member's addiction?

_____

_____

6. Have you ever had a friend who exhibited such Jesus-like behavior that you were drawn to him or her, and ultimately to God? What does that friend mean to you? How has she impacted your spiritual journey?

_____

_____

7. Do you ask God to search your heart? If so, what is the result? What do you do with what gets uncovered?

_____

_____

Epilogue

"And after you have suffered a little while, the
God of all grace, who has called you to His eternal
glory in Christ, will Himself restore, confirm,
strengthen, and establish you." 1 Peter 5:10

Epilogue

The walking wounded surround us daily.
Skewered by loss.
Stabbed by betrayal.
Struck by cancer.
Staggered by abuse.
They limp in pain, at least for a season. Some wander
   aimlessly. Some walk in faith-filled obedience. Some
   barely walk at all.
Even in the depths of despair, we cannot hide from God. The
   Holy Spirit maps the location where we've fallen.
In the midst of charred ruins.
In the hospital bed of illness.
In the dungeon of anger.
In the corner of shame.
On the battlefield of faith.
In the heartbreak of choice.
In the ruins of trust.
In the desperation of addiction.
And God whispers into the pain.

Comfort.

"Comfort, comfort My people, says your God" (Isaiah 40:1).

Our Savior pursues us in love to turn our scars into life-changing stories. To use our discomfort to draw us to Him to receive comfort so that we can learn how to comfort others. For His glory.

As you close the last page of this study, this is my prayer for you:

That you feel fully.

Grieve honestly.

Receive God's divine comfort openly.

Pore through God's Word daily.

Pray fervently.

Worship wholeheartedly.

Allow others to come alongside you unapologetically.

And use your experience to pour comfort into those God places around you.

He redeems your pain and places others around you for a reason.

References

2 Corinthians 1, Logos Research Systems, Libronix, 2007.

Achtemeier, Paul J. *Harper's Bible Dictionary,* Harper & Row Publishers, Logos Research Systems, 2007.

Bible Exposition Commentary, Logos Research Systems, 2007.

BibleGateway.com, 2 Corinthians 1:3–5, Gospel Communications International, ©1995–2008. Accessed November 2, 2011.

Blue Letter Bible. Dictionary and Word Search for hypotassō (Strong's 5293). 1996–2012. http:// www.blueletterbible.org/lang/lexicon/lexicon.cfm? Strongs=G5293&t=KJV. Accessed January 23, 2012.

Blue Letter Bible. Dictionary and Word Search for Mĕphiybosheth (Strong's 4648). 1996–2012. http://www.blueletterbible.org/lang/lexicon/lexicon.cfm? Strongs=H4648&t=KJV. Accessed January 23, 2012.

Carpenter, Eugene and Philip W. Comfort. *Holman Treasury of Key Bible Words.* Nashville, TN: Broadman & Holman Publishers, 2000, pp. 255, 402.

Coffman, James Burton, "Commentary on 2 Corinthians 1," *Coffman Commentaries on the Old and New Testament,* http://www.searchgodsword.org/com. Abilene, TX: Abilene Christian University Press, Abilene, 1974. Accessed November 2, 2011.

Conflict Resolution Education. "Anger: A Secondary Emotion." http://www.creducation.org/resources/anger_management/anger__a_secondary_emotion.html. Accessed January 9, 2012.

Copeland, Mark A. "Executable Outlines": Second Corinthians—Expository Outlines, Christian Classics Electronic Library, 1997. http://wee.ccel.org/contrib/exec_outlines/2cor.htm. Accessed November 2, 2011.

Dictionary.com, "contentment," in Easton's 1897 Bible Dictionary. http://dictionary.reference.com/browse/contentment. Accessed December 18, 2011.

Dommer, Rev. Douglas. "Christmas Love" Bible study on John 3:16, December 2007, Salem Lutheran Church, Tomball, Texas.

Dommer, Rev. Douglas. "Father, Forgive Them" sermon on forgiveness, October 1, 2008, Salem Lutheran Church, Tomball, Texas.

Dommer, Rev. Douglas. "Now What?" sermon on hell, January 27, 2008, Salem Lutheran Church, Tomball, Texas.

Elmblad, Roxanne, member of Salem Lutheran Church, mother of soldier serving in Iraq. Interviewed and quoted by permission.

Henry, Matthew. "Complete Commentary on 2 Corinthians 1." Matthew Henry Complete Commentary on the Whole Bible, http://www.searchgodsword.org/com/mhc-com. Accessed November 3, 2011.

Holman Treasury of Key Bible Words: Greek *parakletos*; Strong's: 3875

Kopp, Heather. "Crimes against Grace," blog post January 18, 2012. www.soberboots.com. Used and quoted by permission from author. Accessed January 18, 2012.

Kopp, Heather. "Damn You, Free Will, I Love You," blog post January 11, 2012, www. soberboots.com. Used and quoted by permission from author. Accessed January 11, 2012.

McGarvey, J.W. and Philip Y. Pendleton, "Commentary on 2 Corinthians," The Fourfold Gospel. Cincinnati, OH: Standard Publishing Company, 1914. http://www. searchgodsword.org/com. Accessed November 5, 2011.

Jamieson, Fausset, and Brown Bible Commentary of 2 Corinthians, e-Word Today electronic version, L. Hodgett, 1995.

Jamieson, Robert; A.R. Fausset; and David Brown. "Commentary on 2 Corinthians 1." Blue Letter Bible. February 19, 2000. 2011. http://www.blueletterbible.org/ commentaries/comm_view.cfm?AuthorID=7&contentID=2990&commInfo=6&top ic=2%20Corinthians&ar=2Cr_1_3. Accessed November 15, 2011.

Lane, Deforia. "The Harmony of Faith and Suffering" (Women's Devotion Bible 2), New International Version®. Grand Rapids, MI: Zondervan, 1995.

"Life Today: Wednesdays with Beth, James and Betty Robison." Daystar Network; air date May 21, 2008.

Kym, Ray, member and Elder of Salem Lutheran Church. Interviewed and quoted by permission.

Niekerk, Kristin L., MS, LPC, Christian psychotherapist. (See Special Acknowledgements).

NIV Study Bible. Grand Rapids, MI: Zondervan, 1995, pp. 1872.

"Reactive Attachment Disorder." http://www.mayoclinic.com/health/reactive-attachment-disorder/DS00988. Accessed December 1, 2011.

Salem Lutheran Church (Tomball, TX) brainstorming team on comfort: Joel Wetzstein, Pam Mintari, Stan Nelson, Matt Werner, Steven Gumke, Peter Burroughs, Jill Carter, Mary Pieper, and Dayna Williams.

Scott, Thomas. "2 Corinthians," The Treasury of Scripture Knowledge, Blue Letter Bible, 1836.

Slick, Matthew J. "Encouragement." Christian Apologetics and Research Ministry, 1996–2006. www.carm.org. Accessed November 1, 2011.

Sulfridge, Jennie, and her daughter, Hannah. Interviewed and quoted by permission.

Thayer's Greek-English Lexicon of the New Testament. Peabody, MA: Hendrickson Publishers, 2005.

The Archeological Study Bible, New International Version®, Grand Rapids, MI: Zondervan, 2005.

The English-Greek Reverse Interlinear New Testament, English Standard Version®. Wheaton, IL: Crossway Books, 2006.

The Leadership Bible, New International Version®. Grand Rapids, MI: Zondervan, 1998. Page 1357

The Strongest Strong's Exhaustive Concordance of the Bible, 21st Century Edition. Grand Rapids, MI: Zondervan, 2001.

Thompson Chain Reference Bible: New International Version. Indianapolis, IN: B. B. Kirkbride Bible Co., Inc., 1990.

Vine's Complete Expository Dictionary of Old and New Testament Words. Nashville, TN: Thomas Nelson Publishers, 1996.

Wetzstein, Joel, director of worship and integrated communications, Salem Lutheran Church, Tomball, Texas. Interviewed and quoted by permission.

Wiersbe's Outline of the New Testament, Logos Research Systems, 2007.

About the Author

A soul-stirring, engaging speaker, author, Bible teacher, and worship leader, Donna Pyle has a passion for studying and teaching God's Word. Her clear, down-to-earth style encourages women of all ages to wholeheartedly love, serve, and live for Jesus Christ.

Not raised going to church regularly, Donna understands how dehydrated life is without Christ's living water. Now, after being baptized and walking with Him for more than twenty years, she anchors deep in His soul refreshment. She loves to mentor and encourage other women who are starting down that same, wonder-filled path of faith.

Since launching Artesian Ministries in 2007, Donna has authored eighteen Bible studies, published several shorter Bible studies in the *Lutheran Woman's Quarterly,* and written numerous devotions and magazine articles. She released her first eight-lesson DVD-based Bible study series, *Your Strong Suit,* in partnership with the Lutheran Women's Missionary League in November 2011. She serves as a staff writer and regular contributor for *Blessed Life Magazine.*

In 2011, Donna signed with literary agent Rachelle Gardner at Books & Such Literary Agency; she is currently working on a nonfiction book.

Donna enjoys blogging about faith-based issues on the Artesian Ministries' blog, "Hydrated Living." She is active on Facebook and Twitter where she connects with family and friends, and she uses our social media–driven age to spread God's love, joy, and hope.

Donna is a member of Salem Lutheran Church in Tomball, Texas, where she serves in the worship ministry and LWML. Donna fuels her creativity with Chick-Fil-A® and Starbucks®. She enjoys writing, traveling, time with family and friends, reading, singing with her church's worship team, and torturing her cats with feather toys.

Artesian Ministries LLC
PO Box 96
Spring, TX 77383
inquiry@artesianministries.org
BLOG: www.hydratedliving.com
Twitter: @DonnaPyleTX

Special Acknowledgements

Rev. Douglas Dommer

An avid student of God's Word and gifted teacher of Scripture, Doug has been an a LCMS ordained minister for over thirty years. He received his associate of arts degree from Concordia University in Austin, Texas, in 1974 and earned a bachelor of science from the University of North Texas in 1977. In 1981, he received his master of divinity from Concordia Seminary in St. Louis, Missouri.

Doug's extensive experience as a pastor and counselor contributed invaluable insights to this study. A fourth-generation LCMS pastor, Doug serves as the pastor of spiritual formation at Salem Lutheran Church in Tomball, Texas (salem4u.com).

Sitting under Doug's gifted teaching for years and witnessing his contagious love for Jesus and rapacious passion to dig deep into Scripture has nurtured my spiritual growth, and has encouraged me to live on God's Word and step out in faith to write and teach Bible studies. It is a privilege to call him and his sweet wife, Delo, dear friends.

Kristin L. Niekerk, MS, LPC

Kristin received her bachelor of arts degree in psychology from Concordia University in Wisconsin and a master of science degree in educational psychology/community counseling from University of Wisconsin-Milwaukee.

As a licensed psychotherapist in both Texas and Wisconsin, Kristin has specialized in treating eating and weight disorders for more than ten years. A lifelong Christian and a pastor's wife, Kristin's approach to treatment focuses on spirituality as the foundation of physical and emotional wellness. She founded Pathway Counseling Services in Tomball, Texas (pathwaycounselingservices.com).

Kristin is the wife of Rev. Timothy Niekerk, an LCMS ordained minister serving as the senior pastor designate at Salem Lutheran Church in Tomball, Texas. With great love, tenderness, and grace, Kristin counseled and worked with me for over a year to sift through painful issues following my divorce. Time and time again, she pointed me to the God of all comfort. Her professional counseling experience provided indispensable depth and insight to this study. She and Tim's precious friendships have blessed me beyond measure.

Notes

Notes